LIVING LITERACIES

LIVING LITERACIES

RETHINKING LITERACY RESEARCH AND PRACTICE THROUGH THE EVERYDAY

KATE PAHL AND JENNIFER ROWSELL

WITH DIANE COLLIER, STEVE POOL, ZANIB RASOOL, AND TERRY TRZECAK

THE MIT PRESS CAMBRIDGE, MASSACHUSETTS LONDON, ENGLAND

This book was set in Avenir by Westchester Publishing Services. Printed and bound in the United States of America.

Library of Congress Cataloging-in-Publication Data

Names: Rowsell, Jennifer, 1969- author. | Rowsell, Jennifer, 1969- author.
Title: Living literacies : rethinking literacy research and practice through the everyday / Kate Pahl and Jennifer Rowsell ; with Diane Collier, Steve Pool, Zanib Rasool, and Terry Trzecak.
Description: Cambridge, Massachusetts : The MIT Press, [2020] | Includes bibliographical references and index.
Identifiers: LCCN 2020000414 | ISBN 9780262539715 (paperback)
Subjects: LCSH: Literacy--Social aspects. | Literacy--Research. | Critical pedagogy.
Classification: LCC LC149 .R69 2020 | DDC 302.2/244--dc23
LC record available at https://lccn.loc.gov/2020000414

10 9 8 7 6 5 4 3 2 1

This book is dedicated to the memory of Brian V. Street (October 24, 1943–June 21, 2017), a utopian scholar who inspired both Kate and Jennifer, and to Gunther Kress (March 18,1940–June 20, 2019), a true visionary who made us see the world differently.

Kate would also like to dedicate this book to the memory of her amazing colleague Lisa Procter (February 13, 1981–November 11, 2017), who passed away during the writing of this book but whose spirit and ideas infuse its pages.

CONTENTS

ACKNOWLEDGMENTS

Kate Pahl would like to thank her wonderful colleagues at Manchester Metropolitan University, in particular Janet Batsleer, Geoff Bright, James Duggan, Abigail Hackett, Liz de Frietas, Gabrielle Ivinson, Deborah James, Maggie MacLure, Christina Macrae, and David Rousell.

Her special thanks to Christian Ehret for reading the "Creating" chapter (chapter 6) and to Elizabeth Campbell, Hugh Escott, Candace Kuby, Joanne Larson, Karen Salt, Anna Smith, Sarah Truman, and Lalitha Vasudevan for their insightful conversations.

Kate would like to thank the "Feeling Odd in the World of Education" project team—Rachel Holmes, Steve Pool, Amanda Ravetz, Becky Shaw, and Alma Park Primary School, Manchester—and the "Imagine" project team, especially Sarah Banks, Angie Hart, and Paul Ward. She joins Zanib Rasool in thanking the "Threads of Time" Utopia Festival project team, especially Shaheen Shah, Helen Mort, and the girls' poetry group, especially Aliya Qaddar, Hafsah Wahid, and Aisha.

Thank you as well from Kate to the "Taking Yourselves Seriously" project team, in particular Andrew McMillan and Josie Webster at Clifton School in Rotherham. Steve Pool would like to thank Patrick Meleady at Pitsmoor Adventure Playground, Sheffield. And Zanib would like to thank Nazia Latif, Mariam Shah, and the 1970s Clifton School cohort of Pakistani women and their mums.

Kate would also like to thank Hugh Escott, Deborah Bullivant, Richard Steadman-Jones, Marcus Hurcombe, and Johan Siebers from the "Inspire Rotherham," "Writing in the Home and in the Street," "Language as Talisman," and the "Communicating Wisdom: Fishing and Youth Work" research projects. And she gives thanks to the Arts and Humanities Research Council (AHRC) and the Economic and Social Research Council (ESRC), Creative Partnerships, and Yorkshire Forward for funding these projects.

Jennifer Rowsell would like to thank her colleagues at Brock University, in St. Catharines, Ontario, in particular Fiona Blaikie, Diane Collier, Dane Di Cesare, Tiffany Gallagher, Shelley Griffin, Deb Harwood, Julian Kitchen, Dolana Mogadime, and Peter Vietgen, for their support, humor, and friendship. Her thanks also go to Cynthia Lewis, Cheryl McLean, Christian Ehret, Sandra Schamroth Abrams, Candace Kuby, Hans Christian Arnseth, and Mark Shillitoe for their help in thinking through ideas central to this book, as well as to Julianne Burgess, Amélie Lemieux, Terry Trzecak, Jennifer Burkitt, Larry Swartz, Melissa Turcotte, Vanessa Crosbie-Ramsay, Tara Markovitch, Glenys McQueen-Fuentes, and Kari-Lynn Winters for the hard work, creativity, and energy they brought to the research studies featured in *Living Literacies*. Jennifer acknowledges the special group of people who took part in the "Rolling in the Deep: Seeing Differently" research study in June–July of 2016. Jennifer would also like to commemorate the memory of Sean. She is grateful to the Niagara Catholic District School Board, the District School Board of Niagara, Start Me Up Niagara, and the Niagara Folk Arts Multicultural Centre for endorsing and supporting the reported research, as well as to Brock University's Social Justice Research Institute, the James Hugh Corcoran Memorial Foundation, the Social Sciences and Humanities Research Council of Canada, and the Canada Research Chair Secretariat for their funding support. And she gives a special tribute to St. Catharines and Welland, Ontario, as key sites that inform the thinking and community spirit of living literacies research in the book.

Finally, Jennifer and Kate are most grateful for the incredible work of coordinators and editors like Ashley Do Nascimento, Elden Yungblut, Jennifer Turner, and Kate Wicker—without whom *Living Literacies* would not exist. And they give heartfelt thanks to Susan Buckley at MIT Press for believing in their vision for the book and shepherding it through.

FOREWORD

Steve Pool

Fifteen years ago, I encountered New Literacy Studies. I was lucky enough to be introduced to the field through working with Kate Pahl and later Jennifer Rowsell. I say working "with" in a very practical sense; I was not interested in their written work, their books or journal papers. I encountered their ideas in the messy, often-frustrating world of trying to find things out about literacy together.

As a birthright dyslexic, I had spent forty years trying to avoid working directly with words. Through introducing me to New Literacy Studies, Kate allowed me to reimagine what could be considered a text. We stood in front of a display case in a museum containing glass objects on small acrylic mounts, images, and words on museum panels. Kate saw the whole case as a single text with multiple potential meanings. But it took me a while to see this, to extend my definition and therefore the potential of what a text could be.

When you first meet Kate, she tells you a foundational story about her Ph.D. study. She explains how she studied young boys in London playing with action figures; how their whispered under-the-breath play worlds create plateaus of meaning, flows of connections. In liberating texts from the page, New Literacy Studies gives us a way to value, to understand, and to reinvent our conception of what literacy is, but also, and more important, what it does.

Jennifer Rowsell's work sets out to ask what New Literacy Studies can do in the world within and beyond education. Not satisfied with a warning shot across the bow of established literacy education, she is a modern-day pirate of multimodality, boarding ships and taking few prisoners.

New Literacy Studies offers us a way to critique what came before, and it affords a robust and now established approach to reading the world differently. There is a problem at the heart of the term "New Literacy Studies" in that it is no longer new; its critique of the old, although not universally accepted, is now part of the canon.

Living Literacies is a timely book. With the passing of Gunther Kress and Brian Street, we have lost two great scholars and friends. Their legacy may be not only in changing the way we look at the uses of literacy but also in inspiring a group of new scholars who situate themselves in the world with the people who use and own language, who write their love and anger on the world in texts that are no longer held between pages. In questioning its own relevance, *Living Literacies* makes an important contribution to the field.

The writing that Kate and Jennifer do together is always at the edge of the field and often moves the fence posts. *Living Literacies* is a messy book; ideas stick to your feet like the surface coating of beer on the carpet of a backstreet bar. Full of contradictions, inspirations, and cul-de-sacs, it is to be read with an open mind and in good faith. A living text is never complete and meaning is never fixed—this book is no exception.

1

WHAT IS LIVING LITERACIES?

Jennifer Rowsell and Kate Pahl

DEFINING LIVING LITERACIES

A living literacies approach to research starts from the ways that meaning is made as people conduct everyday activities. Indeed, it relies as much on more routine, everyday activities like scrolling through Instagram, watching news footage, or listening to music as it does on official, schooled literacy activities like reading, writing, speaking, and listening to lectures. Living literacies involves being in and of the world: we move through and within literacy all the time (see glossary), and the mind, heart, and body of each of us play equal roles in the process.

Seen in this way, "literacy" naturally conflates felt, sensory experiences with more deliberate ways of thinking and knowing. In the past, literacy has often been framed in terms of its performed, communicational, and informational dimensions at the expense of its more hidden, lived, and sometimes intensely affective dimensions (Ehret 2018a; Leander and Boldt 2013; Leander and Wells Rowe 2006). As it is lived and in constant use, literacy flows through people's rites and practices, and its dynamism and vitality rest firmly on thoughts, emotions, movements, materials, spaces, and places. For us, as literacy researchers, literacy comes alive through observations and reflections on the many ways people engage with texts and technologies across varied spaces. We are very much implicated in the process of observing and taking part in living literacies, and our minds and bodies are never the same after working and connecting with people in research sites (Lewis and Tierney 2013). The forces, relations, and connections between researchers, co-researchers, and co-participants change everyone involved. We, each to each, live with and live from the research process. To engage in literacy broadly and fully, and in literacy research specifically, demands that we view from multiple perspectives the ways people call on their own feelings and ways of knowing to complete the varied tasks before them.

A lived literacies approach implies a turn to activism, to hopeful practice, to creativity, to making, to seeing, and to knowing. "Hoping," Creating," "Making," Seeing," and "Knowing" are some of the titles of our chapters, which are oriented as much toward affect (Lewis and Tierney 2013; Leander and Ehret 2019) as they are toward habits of mind (Bruner 1960). And the structure of *Living Literacies* is oriented toward what we can do *with* literacy, *about* literacy, and *for* literacy. We are aware of the huge challenges facing us in the world—climate change, increased concerns about identity, pervasive sexism, nationalism, the rise of racist and Far Right movements, governmental fissures and fractures, and continuing wars. We see our research as profoundly engaged with these challenges. Like the chapters in this book, our studies have often been collaborative and coproduced, and this has given us a wide-angled lens in our explorations.

LIVING LITERACIES THROUGH THE EYES OF THE EVERYDAY

Literacy is about seeing, disrupting, hoping, knowing, creating, and making; we have featured these key aspects of the literacy experience as separate chapters. Looking at literacy through the eyes of the everyday, our living literacies approach is grounded not only in theories concerned with everyday literacies, but also in new theoretical paradigms that point to the importance of feeling, affect, embodiment, and emotion. We have drawn on the methodologies of traditional anthropology, such as those of ethnography, and on artistic methodologies as well, and we have learned much from coproducing with researchers situated in communities, including young people and activists. All of this has enabled us to see literacy through the eyes of those who live it.

Our work draws on New Literacy Studies, which argues that literacy is an everyday social practice and, as such, situated within the purview of anthropology. In their exploration of everyday life, anthropologists rely on participant observation, doing fieldwork in given settings, often for extended periods of time as part of longitudinal studies (Ingold 2014). Our work has been particularly influenced by that of Brian Street, an anthropologist who studied everyday literacy practices, and references to Street's work run throughout this book. In 1984, with the publication of his *Literacy in Theory and Practice*, literacy came to be known more and more as a social and essentially ideological practice. Within a social group, whether an institution, a discipline, a local community, or a grade school class, the use of written language is seen to be guided by a set of shared literacy practices. But, far from abstract cultural models held in people's minds, these practices are embedded in all aspects of their social situations.

Living Literacies aims to gather together research on literacy and to refocus its gaze. Scholars working in new materialist and posthuman paradigms (see glossary) argue that literacy studies need a wider perspective on meaning making, one that moves beyond humans to "more-than-humans" (Truman 2019) and that extends a more expansive view of literacy into objects, the nonhuman, and affect. Although we are cognizant of the recent turn to materialist and posthuman perspectives (Kuby and Gutshall Rucker 2016), our focus is on literacies as *lived*.

Our impetus to write this book comes from our awareness that literacy is more than the sum of its parts: although it can be followed through traces of practices across sites and spaces, literacy is also a concept that can be ontologically constructed from the bottom up. Indeed, to fully understand it, we need to explore what is happening when we read, write, speak, create, make, and live literacy. As David Bloome and Judith Green (2015, 20) explain: "Literacy cannot be separated from what people are doing, how they are doing it, when, where, under what conditions and with whom they are doing it; metaphorically, there is no separation of the dancer from the dance (cf. Yeats 1962)."

This exploration needs to be collaborative and to encompass both the lived reality of moving through the world and the "not yet" and "What if ... ?" emergent understandings of literacy that doing so gives rise to. Although we recognize the importance of university knowledge about language and literacy, it is in the everyday world that we learn from one another, and it is this "learning from" (Ingold 2014) that makes knowing more present, more felt, more embodied, more situated. To articulate more clearly what could be, the "not yet" (Daniel and Moylan 1997), we need to address the emotions that accompany literacies and to show how living literacies could be coproduced to imagine different communities and make them happen. Our work draws on the idea of practice as research (Barrett and Bolt 2010) and on "material thinking" (Carter 2004). We see perceptual understandings about literacy as built up from the ontological understandings of the people we work with, especially children and young people (Escott and Pahl 2017). In the sections that follow, we chart a history to foreground lineages that have brought us to the present day in literacy studies.

LIVING LITERACIES AND INDIGENOUS PEDAGOGIES

There are parallels between the concept of living literacies in the everyday and indigenous pedagogies such as New Zealand's early childhood Te Whariki curriculum, based entirely on the Te Whariki philosophy of the Maori (My ECE Experts 2013–2019). This curriculum, whose central metaphor is the woven mat, has four main principles: empowerment; holistic development; family and community; and relationships—all of which are tied to the notion of living literacies—and five complementary strands that go along with the main principles: well-being, belonging, contribution, communication, and exploration. The Te Whariki curriculum believes in children depending on one another to make meaning and regards each child in his or her own right (My ECE Experts 2013–2019). Living literacies shares similar values, emphasizing that literacy is idiosyncratic, informed by the ways, beliefs, experiences, and ontologies of individual lives.

CONFRONTING THE LITERACIES OF POWER

Our work is crucially concerned with power and with whose voices count in literacy research and why. In *Critical Literacy and Urban Youth*, Ernest Morrell (2008) argues that, to leverage and articulate what they have to say, students need to develop tools to dissect and make sense of the world in new ways. Valerie Kinloch's work (2010) explains how the literacies of place are racialized. She shows how young people can use particular ways to reclaim their space, in this case Harlem, away from gentrification, and how working with them to do so can begin to unpeel the power structures that constrain how their voices are heard.

Critical race theory describes the ways in which racism percolates throughout societies to systematically exclude and define people as "other" in racialized ways (Ladson-Billings and Tate 1995). Drawing on the work of Carol Lee (2003), we acknowledge the need to make power structures visible and to recognize white privilege in literacy education. A living literacies approach deconstructs this privilege and recognizes that knowledge production structures from the global North inadequately account for how knowledge is produced and recognized. Indeed, indigenous scholars have begun to reveal the ways in which knowledge mapping has systematically excluded and marginalized certain communities from knowledge production within academia (Tuhiwai-Smith, Tuck, and Yang 2019). In acknowledging this, we seek to decenter our work away from a central space into a more contingent zone built on learning *with* participants: coproduction and collaboration invite people to become the definers of their worlds. They give rise both to new conceptualizations of literacies, including hip-hop literacies (Richardson 2007) and the felt literacies of neighborhoods (Kinloch 2010), and to ways of knowing that are neither written nor spoken but something in between across gestural, visual, spoken, and written modes (Finnegan 2015).

WALKING IN SPACES AND TRAVELING IN TIME

Literacy is on the move (Norquist 2017), as global and local literacies blur and seamlessly combine in new and evolving forms. Using the word "transliteracies" as a term to describe this development, Amy Stornaiuolo, Anna Smith, and Nathan Phillips (2017, 74) articulate how "literacies are lived, explored, described, analyzed, and enacted in critical and social practices, situated within and across ideological systems and characterized by the movements and interactions of people and things."

In their walks around neighborhoods, scholars like Ronald and Suzanne Scollon (Scollon and Scollon 2003) have identified the nested and signed spatial nature of literacies. Drawing on Henri Lefebvre's theory ([1974] 1991) of space as produced, Kevin Leander and Margaret Sheehy (2004) have determined that literacy practices are not just produced by space; they also produce space. Nearly a decade later, using ecological models to map neighborhoods, Sue Nichols and colleagues (2012) would identify literacy hubs and investigate how these hubs worked, as would Susan Neuman and Donna Celano (2013). Walking as a way of knowing and coming to know the literacies of a place through stories has been developed in collaborative work by Valerie Kinloch (2010) and by Stephanie Springgay and Sarah Truman (2018). And, for their part, cultural geographers and anthropologists have mapped and experienced place in visceral, sensory, and embodied ways (Pink 2009).

Reminded of the importance of revisiting in longitudinal studies (Sefton-Green and Rowsell 2015), we have seen time to be a key focus of literacy studies, providing a lens through which to look at unfolding events and literacies across generations. Indeed, Kate and her co-researcher Aliya Khan (Pahl and Khan 2015) have investigated the ways in which literacies have traveled across generations and been transformed in the process—from an elderly grandmother's material-covered Qur'an to the literacies of *Harry Potter* and A-level psychology textbooks—as has Catherine Compton-Lilly, who lists the four main purposes of longitudinal research:

1. research that provides a depth of information about a particular site, community or issue;
2. research that explores change over time;
3. research that documents and examines trajectories;
4. research that focuses on the construction of ways of being over time. (Compton-Lilly 2015, 218)

Our work acknowledges the importance of extended time within the field to build up understandings with our participants. Recognizing its site-specific nature—Jennifer's in St. Catharines, Ontario, and Kate's in Rotherham and Sheffield, Yorkshire—it focuses on concepts of success and failure over time and how these can be rethought in the light of new conceptual frameworks. Living literacies research across time and space involves issues of mobility and thinking about people on the move, making meaning across contexts and histories (Norquist 2017).

BECOMING (IM)MATERIAL ACROSS SCREENS AND MEDIA

Our work has engaged strongly with the turn to the visual, material, and multimodal (see Pahl and Rowsell 2006, 2010). We recognize that visual ethnography opens up a different kind of research practice, one that can develop lines of inquiry that are coexistent with participants' perceptual frameworks (Pink 2006). We acknowledge the power of multimodal approaches to understanding the shape and form of everyday texts (Maybin 2013). Such approaches enable researchers to encompass the emergent mark making of children's artwork within an understanding of literacy, as Gunther Kress observed in his seminal work *Before Writing* (1997). Abigail Hackett (2014) has identified children running circles in a museum setting as a form of embodied mark making. Tracing literacies across visual maps and geographies means moving into online worlds. Material and (im)material literacies are intertwined in digital worlds (Burnett, Merchant, et al. 2014). Wider frameworks for literacy are needed to make sense of the lived worlds of children and young people, as they engage with digital script and online images on their smartphones and tablets (Burnett 2015).

Digital literacies cut into these spatialities in complex ways. We see the spatial move as young people mash up their daily life in YouTube videos and cross time zones when they send messages across the globe using WhatsApp and SnapChat. These ways of communicating can be apprehended only by paying attention to the located and distant scales of activity. Tracing the scalar movements (Stornaiuolo, Smith, and Phillips 2017; see also glossary) of literacies across the globe can involve being attentive to the "Ariadne's thread" that connects apparently invisible literacies (Brandt and Clinton 2002). Our work, in recognizing these intersecting transliteracies as part of living literacies, highlights the need to attend to their emergence, resonance, uptake, and scale (Stornaiuolo, Smith, and Phillips 2017). We appreciate this transliteracies framework as it focuses on freeze-framing the moments when literacies are taken up, resonate, move, and then emerge in new sites.

Our studies have drawn on the idea of literacy as "worldmaking" (Stornaiuolo 2015), which in itself engenders further creative practices. Literacy events quickly settle into practices as they spread across the globe. Aesthetic understandings offer a sense of how literacies are crafted and shaped and how they emerge through handling over time (Pahl 2014b). Amy Stornaiuolo (2015, 568) describes the role of the imagination in worldmaking:

> One of the most important dimensions of worldmaking is the capacity to imagine. Creativity is at the heart of the semiotic and social work involved in imagining social worlds, and imagination forms the cornerstone of our capacity to agentively shape meaning, especially within asymmetries of power.

We locate the thinking embedded in a worldmaking view within many of the ingredients of *Living Literacies*—in its focus on reaching out, its engaged cosmopolitanism, and its emphasis on young people as makers and creators, for example.

KNOWING DIFFERENTLY—THINKING AND FEELING

> The "doing" of emotions ... is bound up with the sticky relation between signs and bodies: emotions work by working through signs and bodies to materialize the surfaces and boundaries that are lived as worlds.
> —Sara Ahmed (2014, 191)

Our living literacies approach recognizes the role of affect, embodiment, and emotions in the ways people live literacies. Indeed, drawing on work by Christian Ehret (2018b) and Maggie MacLure (2011), we view affect as key to a living literacies approach. Ehret (2018a) argues that, in focusing only on social practices, texts, and what already exists, New Literacy Studies accounts overlook feelings, sensations, and ways of knowing that are foundational to the qualities of meaning. Describing his research in hospitals, he points out the importance of including affect: "Knowing and feeling affective dimensions of literacies as they emerge through the moments ... require speculative propositions that lure us into grasping relational transformations as they happen" (Ehret 2018b, 566).

This produces a speculative concept of "literacy" as "becoming." Ella and Cole, two young people with whom Ehret worked on compositions, think and feel with literacy, working in moment-by-moment ways to transform what literacy could be. Focusing on affect in literacy studies can unsettle ways of knowing and the idea of the autonomous subject (Truman 2019). Discussion of queer literacies gives rise to messy, sticky, and uncomfortable understandings of the exclusions that dominant definitions of literacy can bring (Ahmed 2014). Our vision of literacy, then, is that it can encompass more than representational work; it can include affect, and it can push back at ways of knowing that define the world in particular ways.

HISTORICAL CONTEXT FOR THE BOOK

Living Literacies builds on a tradition that has explored the literacies of the everyday, using mainly ethnographic research methods. In this section, we provide the scholarly historical context for the book and its ideas. To orient readers toward our living literacies approach, we introduce them to the key scholars whose work has influenced ours and describe their contributions to a living literacies approach by revisiting classic accounts of literacy practices in communities.

We start with the work of Shirley Brice Heath, who spent many years in the Piedmont Carolinas documenting community literacy and language practices, drawing on studies of communicative practices developed by the anthropologist Dell Hymes (1996). In *Ways with Words,* Heath (1983, 2) shares a question that led her on the long journey to her historic, groundbreaking study: "What were the effects of preschool home and community environments on the learning of those language structures and uses which were needed in classrooms and job settings?" She lived literacy alongside her research communities in three locations: Trackton (predominantly African American and working class), Roadville (predominantly white and working class), and Maintown (mixed race and predominantly middle class), in South Carolina. Heath not only documented rites and practices related to literacy, but she also unraveled "ways of living, eating, sleeping, worshipping, using space, and filling time" (Heath 1983, 3) that surrounded the communities in which she lived and researched for over a decade. Her book argues that the ways in which children learned to use language in Roadville and Trackton were dependent on the ways in which communities structured families, defined roles, set up spaces, and formed concepts of childhood (Heath 1983, 11). As with all social contexts, legacies solidified at the time informing how children and adults communicated and how literacies were lived.

Through her detailed ethnographic work, Heath gave readers a way into understanding the literacy practices of specific communities in South

Carolina in the 1970s. Although generations of white working-class families in Roadville had changed over the years, there were certain commonalities that stretched across their past, prominent among them religion and religious activities, doing for oneself by sewing, woodwork, crafts, gardening, and maintaining a home. And there were also paradigmatic assumptions—men were the breadwinners, paychecks were devoted to running the home, and a home had to have a garden that was harvested every year. The African American working-class families in Trackton had their own codes of behavior, habits, and values that shaped the ways that they lived their lives and made meaning. There were generational patterns, with respectable people and "no-accounts" and transients. The no-accounts were often linked with respectable families, but they had fallen in with the wrong crowd or had made poor life choices. Trackton residents hated the notion of welfare or being regarded as poor. Though the outsides of their houses were frequently run-down, the interiors were highly decorated, filled with valued artifacts and supplies. In Trackton as in Roadville, there were gender divides, with women rearing children and working on the fields and men working at the mill and having to move north and send money back home. Heath chronicled these habits, rites and practices, and demonstrated time and again in her groundbreaking book that literacy is lived deeply and richly across communities.

Heath's descriptions of community lives offered readers a way to appreciate connections between actions and habits as well as more profound ways of knowing. Her documenting how disparate people practiced literacy in the everyday gave researchers new ways of documenting the development of language and communication skills across communities of use.

To better understand how literacy is entangled within people's everyday, we need to revisit Heath's concept of a "literacy event," which she defines as an occasion when written text and talk around text create interpretations and meanings and often lead to other types of text, where "text" plays a diverse and expansive role that can involve talk, listening, written texts, and pictures (Heath 1983, 22; see also glossary). Street (1995, 2) extended this work by describing social and linguistic practices that encompass literacy events: "The concept of literacy practices is pitched at a higher level of abstraction and refers to both behavior and the social and cultural conceptualizations that give meaning to the uses of reading and/or writing." A modern-day literacy practice could be adding comments or liking a comment on social media. The idea of the "literacy event" has been rethought in chapter 7 to include the processes and affect behind the event. Closely researching literacy practices as they emerge in the world provides a complex and nuanced understanding of literacy as in-process (Ehret 2018b).

The work of Dell Hymes, who documented linguistic practices of communities, was influential in forming our ideas about what language and literacy mean in the everyday. In Hymes's ethnographies, he strove to focus on how ordinary life is practiced, extending the concept of "literacy" into "what every human being must do" (Hymes 1996, 13). Hymes stressed the importance of the interdependence of the general and the particular; he showed how the layers and complexities within communities should be thought of not as single languages, but instead as "repertoires of language" practiced across contexts (Hymes 1996, 33). In the "Warm Springs Interlude," he noted that, within indigenous linguistic habits, there is a building up of narratives about specific events over time; that "experience becomes an event by being told and retold and it eventually takes shape into a narrative" (Hymes 1996, 116); and that performance and language are braided together within such moments, when "incidents, even apparently slight incidents, have pervasively the potentiality of an interest that is worth retelling" (Hymes 1996, 118). This example, drawing on lived experience, enables us to consider the relationship between culture and literacy through lived engagement with practice.

Literacy is not a separate set of skills, stripped of meaning, but located within social practices. From his fieldwork in Iranian villages in the early 1970s, Street (1984) came to understand the ideologically situated nature of literacy. What began to emerge as literacy practices were uses and meanings of literacy around three domains of social activity: *maktab* literacy practices, associated with the primary Qur'anic school; schooled literacy practices in the more secular and modernizing context of the state school; and commercial literacy practices associated with buying and selling fruit for transport to the cities and the markets (Street 1984, 133). The practices in this third domain were quite different from those in either of the other two. Characterizing these domains of social activity as literacy practices helped Street to understand their differences, and he could then articulate whether there were certain identities associated with particular practices. Thus the identity associated with maktab literacy was derived from traditional authority in the village located in Qur'anic learning and with a social hierarchy dominated by men, whereas schooled literacy was associated with new learning and with modernization, leading some village children to urban lives and jobs. And commercial literacy emerged in response to the economic activity of selling fruit to the nearby cities at a time of economic boom and involved writing notes, checks, lists, names on crates, and so on to facilitate the purchase and sale of quantities of fruit.

The framework for understanding literacy that Street (1984) was developing at this time, which included the concept of "literacy practices," aimed to explain why commercial literacy was mainly undertaken by those who had been taught at the Qur'anic school rather than by those taught at the modern state school, even though we might expect the literacy skills of the latter to be more functionally oriented to commercial practices. Here again a living literacies approach shows literacy bubbling up into so many different aspects and spaces of life and living. Where Qur'anic school literacy offered status and authority to carry on commercial practices, state school literacy lacked a grounding in the local and everyday village life. These were distinctly different approaches to language development and making meaning—both equally embedded within daily lives. In this village context, then, literacy was not simply a set of functional skills, as much modern schooling and many literacy agencies represent it, but rather a set of social practices deeply associated with identity and social position.

We argue in this book that literacy is too important to be reduced to a set of skills. The distorting focus on skills privileges classed and raced versions of what literacy is; it perpetuates and shores up future inequalities. Instead, with Street (1993a), we argue that literacy is ideologically situated within power and discourses. Typically circulating within autonomous top-down models of literacy and curricula, however, the reductionist definitions of literacy in Western schooling, based on book learning, are held as the gold standard for literacy success to this day.

The difficulty with such thinking is that it takes no account of contexts and the idiosyncratic nature of people's lives and stories. And, more important, its autonomous models of literacy, rooted in white, middle-class belief systems about success and achievement, marginalize the rich and varied lived literacies that we foreground in these chapters. The research we present concentrates on literacies as historically situated sets of social practices that are highly dependent on what people *do* with literacy. Rendered without its lived dimensions, literacy continues to support positions of power and rhetoric about "the average student" (i.e., middle class and white). Our work acknowledges and challenges the implicit bias that treats students who do not speak or write standardized versions of literacy and language as "other," and we argue that public renderings of literacy are inextricably linked to power relations that need unpacking.

A foremost thinker on the role of texts in the everyday is Mary Hamilton, who talks about texts as "woven into everyday patterns of social practice in locally specific ways" (Hamilton 2012, 2), and who finds that the textual patterns people develop over time are dependent on linguistic and cultural contexts and the availability of materials and technologies. Although there is a dynamism about these interwoven patterns, there are also disparities and power issues to consider. Hamilton (2012) pushes for examining narratives that circulate in texts as the politics of representation. Such work demands that literacy researchers analyze how public narratives emerge in media and social domains and how people mobilize them. Extending this further, researchers need to locate these public narratives within the broader cultural narratives that feed into what is thought of as literacy. Hamilton points to connections between the "social imaginary" of Charles Taylor and the role of literacy in society: "The social imaginary is that common understanding that makes possible common practices and a widely shared sense of legitimacy" (Taylor 2004, 23).

The concept of a social imaginary, namely, work that engages with communities and common cultural lives, has emerged in literacy studies through ethnographic research (Barton and Hamilton 2000; Bloome and Green 2015; Larson and Moses 2018; Pahl 2014a). Ethnography enables researchers to successfully couple more official, institutional approaches to literacy with more informal and vernacular types of literacy. This more expansive vantage point allows them not only to uncover the ebb and flow of agendas and discourses, but also to foreground what Deborah Brandt (2001) calls the "sponsors of literacy." In *Literacy in American*

Lives (2001), Brandt finds that these sponsors play a critical role in the infrastructure of support for literacy, lending their resources to people to promote their literacy development, but also benefiting themselves because the "sponsored" carry the ideological weight of the learning that accompanies that development (Brandt 2001, 17–21). Brandt and Katie Clinton (2002) have identified the ways that texts carry links that can reach beyond local contexts; within the idea of literacy sponsors lies their argument about the inextricable relationship between the local and the global in texts, namely, that literacy has to be regarded within a larger global framework so that people can exist in the local but communicate across global spaces (Brandt and Clinton 2002; see also Kell 2006).

In *Living Literacies*, we consider the relationship between local spaces, where, for example, the voices of girls and women are sometimes lost within more global arenas of power. We argue that, to create equitable structures, we also need to reconstitute how knowledge structures are developed. Ways of knowing that do not honor people's crafted understandings risk undercutting and disempowering their knowledge. In our scholarship, we recognize the need to realign with those who are not listened to and, standing together with them, to articulate their concerns.

METHODOLOGY MATTERS

Our book rests on the argument that, to see literacy as lived, researchers need to capture the process of living literacy. We argue that a living literacies approach rests on a reflexively alive mode of researching, in which the process of "coming to know" is entangled within the research ideas. As Cheryl McLean (2019, 105) explains: "It is through the coming together of the social, cultural, and material worlds, and our collective *experiencing* of these worlds, that we fully come to know our research in the field."

A living literacies approach is generated through the sites and spaces of the literacy projects undertaken. Collaborative and interdisciplinary by nature, it enables artists, community partners, and researchers to work together in a more entangled way while acknowledging and foregrounding expertise that comes from different spaces. This might entail facilitating discussions around research approaches that lead to multiple outputs, such as exhibitions, artworks, and cocreated books. It means focusing less on research articles that are inaccessible to people with no access to university libraries—and that may be written in language unfamiliar to them. Ideas for living literacies projects are determined and built up with communities. Outputs include exhibitions, coauthored books, and artistic products such as poetry. Grounded in emergence, a living literacies approach to research is also relational. Its research processes are embodied and involve people's affect and stories and seeing literacy events through new eyes. The visions research projects give rise to can fracture and disrupt settled ways of knowing.

In our studies, we engaged with coproduction and collaboration in interdisciplinary contexts (Facer and Pahl 2017) to create an expansive view of literacy that draws from the social sciences as well as from the arts and humanities—and specifically from collaborative ethnography (Campbell and Lassiter 2010, 2015) together with co-inquiry and dialogic co-analysis (Banks and Armstrong et al. 2014). We recognize the situated nature of knowledge being built up within projects, and we appreciate that people are differently positioned in terms of their expertise, drawing on a communities-of-practice approach (Hart et al. 2013). We have worked with community practitioners, historians, and artists and have used arts methodologies to develop a way of thinking not contained within university disciplinary structures (Pente et al. 2015; Facer and Pahl 2017). Our research projects are lived and have their own synergy; those involved in them are not objects of study but colleagues, students, artists, and practitioners who cocreate our thinking. Our more grounded approach to research emphasizes the local, the relational, and the situated.

We have seen how researchers such as Shirley Brice Heath and Brian Street positioned literacy in a new way, within the lives of participants. The understandings of these researchers rest on a reflective understanding of who they were in the field (Grenfell and Pahl 2019). Literacy research becomes a process of coming to know, inflected by the self and its own stories:

> The field of literacy and language ethnographical research in general needs not only to understand what knowledge is produced but also who is producing it, and how it is framed and presented. It is here that the tensions around issues of identity/voice, of story/storyteller, speaker/listener, insider/outsider and producer/product, bring into focus the power, the politics and the ethics of our various identities and positionalities and the struggles involved in navigating the patterns and normative practices of our sociocultural contexts (McLean 2019, 104).

One of the key contributions of *Living Literacies* is to produce a coauthored account of literacy developed with co-researchers who have long experience with communities. This has altered our understanding of literacy as a practice both of writing and of knowing. In our previous coauthored books (e.g., Campbell et al. 2018), coauthorship came to the fore as an affirmation of joint scholarship rooted in communities: "Co-production across this book takes many forms—it is enacted in exhibitions, books, discussions, projects, ideas and this book. It offers a way of expanding what 'counts' as knowledge, beyond that which is produced in universities" (Campbell et al. 2018, 207).

Our joint voices emerge from our work on *Living Literacies* and entwine with literacy theory to produce new theories of what literacy could be. Although this creates ripples in the smoothness of our writing, it also expands our definitions and understandings of what literacy could be, in the writing and making of the projects, and in the writing of this book.

WRITERS OF THE BOOK

Our work in schools and communities increasingly rests on collaborations between artists, mental health practitioners, teachers, young people, and diverse groups of scholars and activists. No longer thinking that we "know" how to do literacy research, we live our research projects alongside our collaborators. Our work is dispersed across teams and across sites. As a result, this book is a team effort, and we wish to acknowledge the following partners in our thinking:

Julianne Burgess has taught English as an "additional language" for more than twenty years in settlement and academic settings. A doctoral student at Brock University in St. Catharines, Ontario, and an emerging scholar in literacy and language education, Julianne has conducted four research studies with Jennifer and copublished several pieces with her.

Diane Collier is a scholar who conducts research in the areas of multimodalities and literacies with a special interest in connections across home and school. Using qualitative and ethnographic case studies, Diane interprets how children use everyday resources drawn from popular culture and transmedia worlds to produce multimodal texts. Imbued with ethics and an account of backgrounds and social class, her work has deepened understandings about children and their capacity for creativity and agentive play (see glossary). In chapter 5, on knowing, Diane and Jennifer consider a six-month research study in an elementary school classroom in the Niagara region of Ontario exploring the complicated but important sharing and production of photography as children's contemporary visual literacy practice.

Kate Pahl has worked since 2006 as an ethnographic researcher in Rotherham, a small Yorkshire town outside Sheffield that has experienced the devastation of deindustrialization. She now works in Manchester. She has undertaken a number of collaborative projects funded by the Arts and Humanities Research Council (AHRC) Connected Communities program that have explored literacy and language in everyday life (Pahl 2014a). Her work has connected to everyday ways of seeing and knowing, particularly in relation to coproduction as a methodology. Her most recent projects include the five-year "Imagine" project, which explored the cultural context of civic engagement, and the "Taking Yourself Seriously" project that explored arts methodologies for social cohesion.

Steve Pool is an artist whose practice adjusts to sites and situations, working fluidly within each site to watch and grow with the situation (Pool and Pahl 2015). His work has been created in parks, schools, playgrounds, community halls, and with children, young people, and practitioners to reconstitute the ways in which meanings can be articulated within communities (Pahl and Pool 2011). Steve is currently working on a doctorate on residency as method.

Zanib Rasool is a scholar and activist who has developed her own understandings of community collaborative research (Rasool 2017), using poetic inquiry to look at the lived literacies of young women living with racism in Rotherham. Her work has taught us that literacies are lived, across generations, and within people's stories and poems (Rasool 2019).

Jennifer Rowsell has conducted research in communities in Australia (Nichols, Rowsell, et al. 2012), Canada (Rowsell and McQueen-Fuentes 2017; Rowsell and Vietgen 2017), and the United States (Pahl and Rowsell 2010; Rowsell 2013), applying multimodal approaches to meaning making across a spectrum of modes from photography, to film, to movement. Working closely with professionals in the creative and media arts industries alongside educators, Jennifer researches across age groups from children to adults to observe people's ways of knowing as they engage in compositional practices through arts, digital methodologies, and multimodal approaches to sense making.

Terry Trzecak is an emerging scholar who has developed a methodological approach to data collection that she calls "conscious photography as embodied reflective practice." She has applied this approach across her research and uses it with soldiers in her current doctoral research. Jennifer and Terry applied conscious photography with a group of adults with mental health issues as a part of a six-week research study in the Niagara region that they feature in chapter 2.

With these collaborations in mind, we express our agency in different ways, which allows us to also recognize the multiplicity of perspectives that a living literacies approach entails.

ABOUT THE BOOK

We have conceptualized *Living Literacies* as an active space, with seeing, disrupting, hoping, knowing, creating, and making as key lenses through which we describe and structure our living literacies approach. These lenses are derived from our research projects and, taken together, develop an ontological perspective on literacy as entwined with the world and active within it. Our work is located in people's own ways of knowing.

SEEING

We begin in chapter 2 with seeing, which is where we enter the world, with apprehensions of the visual. We understand seeing as a form of sensory engagement with the world that can reflexively resituate literacies within a wider framework (Pink 2009). Seeing involves memory and the imagination. We see the world through many different kinds of optics. In this chapter, taking photographs becomes a way of seeing the world in a different way—almost like seeing the local from a reimagined perspective. It is about seeing the accretions in layers of ourselves and others in sites. It is the stickiness of seeing that informs our understanding (Ahmed 2004). Seeing starts the journey into living literacies as a practice of reimagining meaning making.

DISRUPTING

In chapter 3, we introduce the literacies of activism, drawing on a community development approach to coproduction that sees collaborative work as a kernel for activist discourses to be nurtured and developed (Banks et al. 2019). The literacies of disrupting involve a focus on moments of dissensus (Rancière 2010) where it is not possible to agree, and they recognize the ways in which activist stances are not always resolvable. Chantal Mouffe (2007) argued that disagreement was important and that there were issues surfacing that could not be resolved within communities. Mouffe called the process of engaged, purposeful disagreement "agonism" (see also glossary) and argued for a politics that incorporated differences as well as similarities. This involved a process of recognizing what differences are. Our work in Rotherham had this quality and acknowledged the ways in which difference can be brought to bear on living literacies (Campbell et al. 2018).

HOPING

In chapter 4, we see our work as being held in the moment, with a sense of what "could be" immanent within that moment. Recognizing coproduction as a utopian vision (Bell and Pahl 2018), we are also mindful of the ways in which a coproduced approach can let in new kinds of knowledges, discourses, and practices that can lead us forward. Hope is part of the process of creating a living literacies approach to research. In this chapter we look at examples where "forward dreaming" (Bloch [1954] 1986) creates new possibilities for literacy and how community narratives can be reconfigured.

KNOWING

In chapter 5, knowledge work by children is seen through their mediations and remixing of images. It is based on a family photos research study that involved reconstituting and reframing family photographs to map out knowledge work. The argument put forth in this chapter is that children make meaning naturally across print and digital spaces, and, in doing so, they enter an imaginative state that allows for making and for new ways of knowing. Using arts and crafts, online and digital tools, children created multimodal compositions and collages from family photos to tell particular stories. Co-researchers Diane and Jennifer note how semiotic resources and recurrent motifs traveled across the group through their arts-based practices.

CREATING

In chapter 6, we consider "What if … ?"—What if the literacy event could be understood differently? What would happen if we viewed the literacy event as a creative act? Drawing on the work of Christian Ehret (2018b), we expand the idea of the event to include coming into being, taking in emotion, affect, and experience. Creation is storied and brings in new stories. In this chapter, the transformative aspect of creativity is considered by Zanib Rasool in her exploration of how artists can shape and be shaped by communities.

MAKING

In chapter 7, Jennifer looks at research studies that were part of a larger project in the Niagara region entitled "Maker Literacies," as well as research with adult refugees engaged in maker work. Examining scholarship on the maker movement and maker approaches, she provides an alternative framing to making by incorporating work on affect and posthumanism. This chapter foregrounds posthuman and new materialist approaches to the ways in which individuals become through materialities and the stickiness (Ahmed 2004) that results from film work. The chapter explores making to know and knowing how to make to illustrate the ways that making and designing are central to a living literacies approach.

LITERACY AS A VERB AND A NOUN

Fundamental to applying living literacies is enacting what we describe and illustrate in chapters 2 and 5, which explore the ideas of "seeing" and "knowing," which involve apprehending, being, and thinking within physical spaces such as streets, art galleries, and classrooms, as well as imagined spaces. Experience is both with and without space and time, so it can be seen as similar to finding part of yourself or your sense of agency in a still-life photograph. In this way, the notion of identity and place are intuitive ideas that can be drawn out with multimodal, digital, and arts-based methodologies. There is a constant flow of material and immaterial influences on our lives that play out in the compositions we make and think through, whether on pages or screens, which have helped us to have conversations with participants and to analyze texts.

Planning material engagements in formal and informal spaces facilitates a moving in and out of material and immaterial worlds. In figure 1.1, the visual presents the idea of literacies both as lived and active but also as a theoretical construct. We see the ideas of "seeing," "knowing," and "making" as offering new theoretical positions on literacy. Literacy is seen in these chapters as woven in with the mode of seeing; it encompasses both the visual and the oral, and the storied. In the "Knowing" chapter (chapter 5), ideas of knowing emerge from an engagement with the visual that produce varied literacy practices. In the "Making" chapter (chapter 7), felt and embodied experiences of wonder and aesthetics combine with a craft approach to produce a maker literacies perspective. Braiding ideas together, these chapters, which position literacy differently, make it possible to "see" literate activities in things that might not appear to be about literacy.

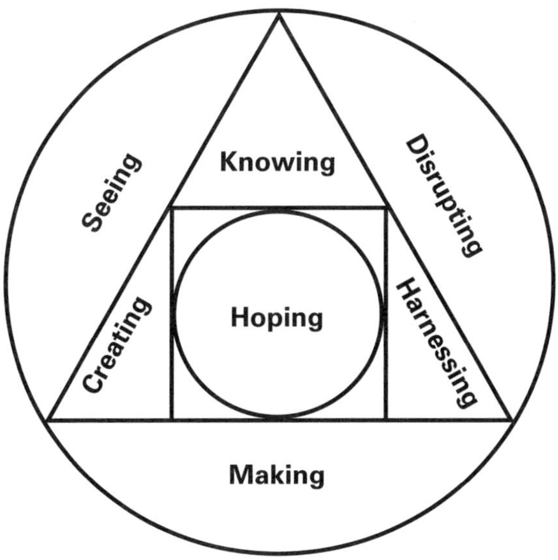

Figure 1.1
Visual for living literacies approach. *Image credit:* Steve Pool

In the "Disrupting," "Hoping," and "Creating" chapters (chapters 3, 4, and 6), the emphasis is on action. By disrupting and activism, literacy can be changed to include a wider array of practices that include exchanging information at a school gate or decorating a Union Jack. By contrast, creating offers a vision of literacy as disruption—by seeing the literacy event as a point of interruption, its creative power comes into play. Hoping is a stance that offers a forward-looking view of literacy, as "not yet" and resting in what is to come. We see these chapters as verbs or as methodological waymarks guiding the route to a living literacies approach. Our vision is encoded in the visual of figure 1.1, which shows how the core ideas of "seeing," "making," and "knowing" are amplified by the doing and thinking of "hoping" and "creating." Within chapters 2 through 7 lie the practice and methodological shifts that are required for a living literacies approach.

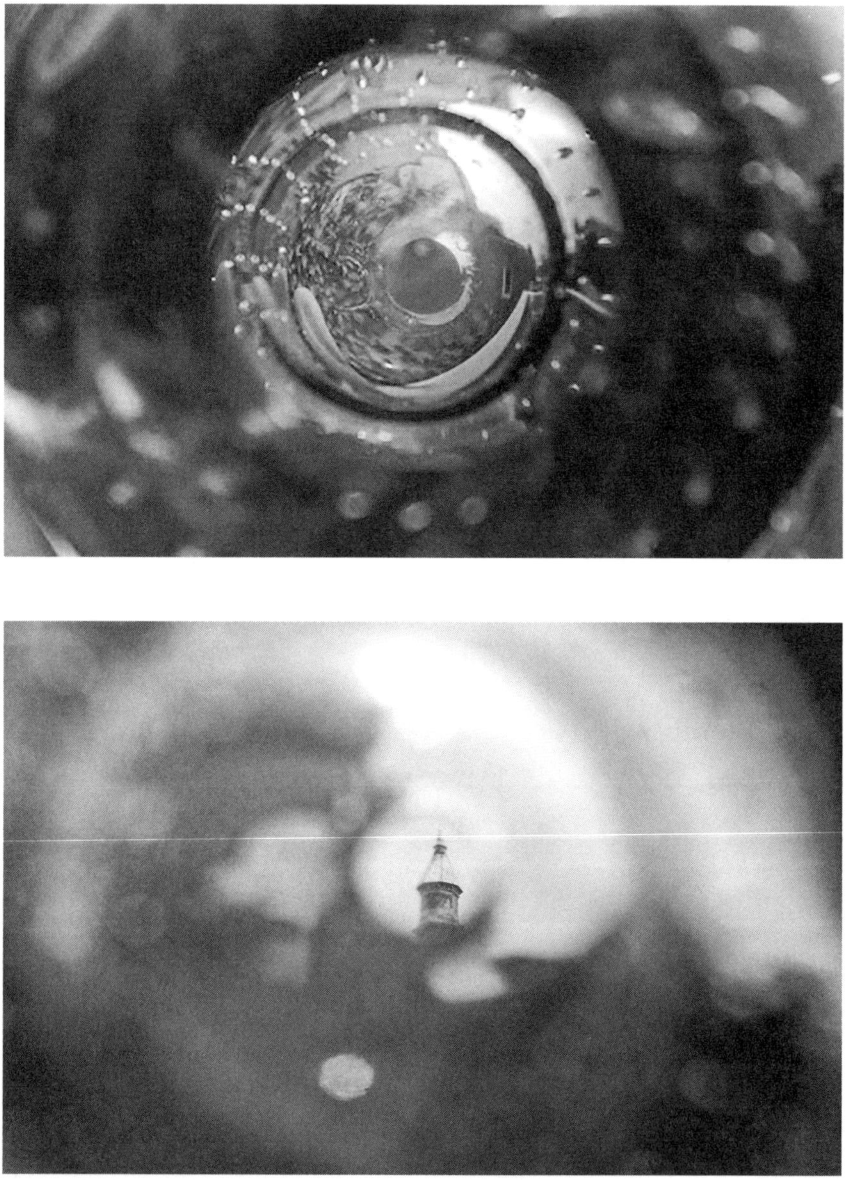

Figure 2.1
"Paperweight" by Emily, shown from above (top) and with a building steeple as viewed through the paperweight.

2

SEEING: LIVING LITERACIES AS A PERCEIVED PRACTICE

Jennifer Rowsell and Terry Trzecak

A way of seeing is also a way of not seeing.
Kenneth Burke (1954, 40)

WHY SEEING IS A LIVED LITERACY PRACTICE

This chapter looks at seeing as a way of pushing against a representational focus on design in literacy research (Leander and Boldt 2013) and of focusing on literacy as a more embodied, affectively driven process (Ehret 2018b)—a way of reimagining what literacy can be. Drawing on "Rolling in the Deep: Seeing Differently," a six-week research project in June–July of 2016 with eleven adults who had experienced trauma, addiction, and mental health struggles (see "Chapter 2 featured study" in appendix), the chapter demonstrates how seeing worlds through a camera lens close-up, at angles, and through objects can shift perspectives and help people realize that seeing is a deliberate, felt process. From their experience with formal schooling, project participants had tended to think of literacy learning as a skills-based, performative process. Taking photos of places, objects, and landmarks helped them recast visual literacy work from instrumental, performative tasks to more meaningful, even ideological work (Street 1995).

When people observe literacy in the everyday and walk the streets to document literacy practices in street signs, graffiti, posters, leaflets, and inscriptions, literacy looks different (Scollon and Scollon 2003); such observations engender an ecological, situated view of literacy. Chapter 1 reviews the work of key New Literacy Studies scholars who have engaged in similar work (Barton and Hamilton 1998; Heath 1983; Street 1995). Building on this important work, in this chapter, our situated account of literacy focuses on a community in southeastern Canada near the border with the United States.

SEEING WHAT COULD BE

The chapter looks at seeing from both a literal and a metaphorical perspective. What people know and believe affects the way they see things (Berger 1972). In this chapter, these two aspects of seeing play out. Although the six-week research project by no means transformed the lives of its participants, there was a noticeable difference in the ways they saw things afterward. It is fair to say that seeing became a hopeful practice for them. Seeing through a series of photographic exercises, practices, and activities—through their entanglements and specifically their direct sensory engagement with objects in the world—gave them a new way to interpret and understand what they were seeing. Taking close-up, landscape, aerial, or distant (long) shots of scenes and things redistributed their agency—blurring relations and intra-actions between human and more-than-human worlds (Barad 2007). Seeing thus became a new way for them to reflect on environments and communities in a contrastive light.

Seeing a familiar community artifact within literacy work can revive and bring forth emplaced memories from the past, and it can project into the future, whereby new promise is seen in familiar settings and locations. Taking a bird's-eye, and even a microscopic, view of environments throws not only humans into relief, but also things, artifacts, and matter itself in those environments. In her photography, Terry avoids taking images of people, instead focusing in on what surrounds people and often goes unnoticed or unremarked. So it is that project participants took many photographs of random things, sites, landmarks, and architectural features. Seeing can be about nonhuman or posthuman literacies (Kuby and Gutshall Rucker 2016) that are unconnected to humans and connected to matter, and the camera provided an "othered" gaze that focused more on matter.

Some seeing is about the primacy of the material world and the vibrancy of the stuff within it (Bennett 2010). In taking a living literacies approach, the foregrounding of material worlds makes seeing about both humans and more-than-humans (Kuby and Rowsell 2017) and reveals the entanglements of people and matter. A living literacies approach invites an account of sociocultural practices across sites while also accounting for the stuff that matters to people (Miller 2008).

RESEARCH CONTEXT

Situated in the Niagara region of Ontario, the research took place in St. Catharines, a midsized blue-collar border city of predominantly white, working-class, single-parent, and two-parent households with some ethnic diversity. There have been more recent efforts to strengthen the infrastructure of the region by making struggling towns and cities like St. Catharines hubs for new business sectors. And, although there has been a slow and steady influx of newcomers engaging in the arts, media, and film, the city continues to struggle with unemployment and housing issues, and a growing number of its residents suffer from addiction and mental illness (Niagara Connects 2014). Some of the many efforts by provincial, federal, and private funders to support those afflicted by poverty, mental illness, and addiction have funded community hubs such as drop-in centers, where individuals seeking help and support come for food, therapy, companionship, and educational opportunities. To conduct the research, our team (see appendix) worked closely with the director of one such drop-in support center to plan and convene an arts-based series of learner units for the study's eleven adult participants.

THE RESEARCH: ROLLING IN THE DEEP

Terry is a researcher and photographer who uses photography as a way of thinking through worlds. Focusing on objects and not on people, Terry sees photography as a contemplative practice rather than an invasive one.

Our research study involved three consecutive arts/multimodal projects: (1) photographing objects and community landmarks or places; (2)

combining movement exercises with storytelling; and (3) play building and mask making. Each project spanned two weeks and was led by an artist (Terry—photography; Glenys McQueen-Fuentes—movement; and Kari-Lynn Winters—play building and mask making) alongside Jennifer, a community support worker, and an arts liaison (see appendix for more research details). The research study started with Terry asking participants to take photographs of everyday objects and community artifacts from a variety of angles and directions. Glenys then asked them to use movement to see otherwise and to create a series of movement tableaux. And Kari-Lynn asked participants to write short plays about homelessness and addiction, and to create masks premised on these stories. Over the study's six weeks, each daily session followed the same schedule. We began at 1 p.m. in either an art gallery or an arts faculty building and then gathered in an opening circle, where someone in the group shared a thought for the day. Following this, there were instructions and activities; and we ended at 3 p.m. with a sharing circle, where participants reflected on what they experienced that afternoon.

The title of our research project is taken from an Adele song, inspired by the British phrase "rolling deep"—having people who look out for you or "have your back."[1] A member of our research team, Aaron Wagner, introduced the song title as a possible project title because he felt that we rolled up our sleeves and rolled in creativity and sense making. It stuck and became our mantra.

Terry envisaged a research project that focused on individual participants' subjective experiences of consciously photographing objects. Deliberately avoiding making images of people allowed the always observant mental health coordinator to gently monitor participants' image making and to intervene to work through any strong emotions as the need arose. Given the wide range of participants' addiction and mental health challenges, there were many emotional moments, and affect coursed through our work together.

Images produced as a part of the research study often evoked painful memories that arose in the process of taking photographs and in

---

1. In an interview with *Rolling Stone* on February 17, 2011, which appeared in the April 28 issue (pp. 30–35), Adele talks about the inspiration behind the title "Rolling in the Deep."

the photographs themselves. Participants took photos of objects like the paperweight pictured at the beginning of the chapter. Of the two images of the paperweight, one simply captures the paperweight itself as seen from above (figure 2.1a), and the other (figure 2.1b) is a conceptual shot of the steeple of an iconic St. Catharines building as seen through the paperweight. The objects photographed by the participants became symbols or metaphors of life stories. They carried what Terry calls "story fractals"—parts of stories as yet untold that materialized in the photographs. Fractals in nature are never-ending patterns, like those in a snowflake or pinecone, which have the same pattern endlessly repeated in ever smaller iterations. Fractals are dynamic: they are always in process, cycling infinitely, one within another. At the beginning of the study, Terry analyzed fractals within her own photographs, asking the group to identify what an object was when seen in a telescopic view. Terry showed a slide show to the group with close-ups of oil in water, rusted pipes, plastic tubes, spiderwebs, and a bird's feather. For many of these images, participants were unsure what they were looking at. Fractals became a motif in the photographs that they took, and the breaking apart and zooming in provided a "cathartic modality" of expression that allowed individuals to see their lives differently. Getting a close-up or a bird's-eye view of objects let them see beauty in the mundane. For instance, during her daily walk, the black flowers that Margaret passed every day without a second thought were transformed into a beautiful work of art.[2] Fractal photos telescoped into objects or places allowing participants to exploit material properties such as color, texture, size, and contrast within visual compositions. When they critically analyzed photographs as a group (which we did at the end of each day), it became clear that the recurrent patterns, as in-process repetitions, revived memories and stories about participants' lives, which they shared with the group and elaborated on during the sharing circle.

Subjectively pulling forth and focusing on an object's inherent properties of contrasting line, color, and texture led participants to produce extraordinary images. Transforming chosen objects into things of personal significance gave them a space to reimagine and to "restory" their

2. Throughout Living Literacies, research participants are called by the assumed first names (pseudonyms) they chose for themselves whenever they wished to have their identities protected.

lives, taking seriously our call for them to "see everydayness in a new light." This practice is similar to that of community researchers who travel through neighborhoods taking photos (Pink 2011), recognizing and highlighting that they live in a sea of words, signs, and artifacts that count as living literacy and are fundamental to their lives.

Crucial to our work in "Rolling in the Deep" was a commitment to materials as relational objects (Hultman and Lenz Taguchi 2010), as opposed to relying on direct human interactions. Thus posthumanism and new materialism lay at the heart of our research project. The object focus aligned so well with our research mission because it avoided any kind of performance or collaboration, which necessarily occurs when photographing people (Shusterman 2012). The mission for participants had to be safe, non-invasive, and free from judgment. Through visual image making, this object focus provided a sense of relationalty, which helped bring participants' stories almost to the surface, so that the as yet untold stories were immanent within the process (Ehret 2018b).

PULLING TOGETHER STRANDS AND "PLUGGING IN" THEORY

Over the course of the research study, Jennifer took ethnographic field notes (Tilley 2016); she and Terry collected significant research artifacts and video footage and interviewed all participants. From the start, our research team adopted what Soyini Madison (2011) describes as a "critical ethnographic approach," characterized by an openness to the research process, in which we documented the research culture and literacy practices and discussed the research with participants. We also worked closely with the community support worker/therapist and the arts liaison, debriefing for an hour after each day's session. The research involved extensive conversations about mental health and addiction and how these factors played a role in arts-based and multimodal practices and assignments. Sessions had a vibrancy to them that responded to the participants' moods, physical states (whether or not they were under the influence of drugs, alcohol, or both), any lingering tensions (from or outside of our research), and mental health conditions. Because this vibrancy was fluid and unpredictable, the mental health worker played an instrumental role in our research process. Moments arose when we had to decide whether particular participants should drop out of the research study for their own personal or mental health benefit, or for a wide range of other reasons, many beyond the research itself. This explains why we started with a group of twenty participants but wound up with a group of eleven.

Eventually, given the in-process and fluid nature of the research study, we decided to adopt a thinking-with-theory approach to coding data (Jackson and Mazzei 2012). Our data analysis was also informed by post-structural theorizing based on the work of Elizabeth Adams St. Pierre (2011) and others, which brought an openness to how we interpreted our participants' affective and embodied responses to image work, movement work, and sculpting with clay and papier-mâché. Thus, in our meetings after daily sessions, we (Terry, Jennifer, and the two support workers) asked questions such as: What affective intensities (Massumi 2015; see also glossary), if any, did we witness in our participants? In what ways was the arts-based work relational, solitary, or both? What were the limitations and affordances of arts materials? Did participants talk about their lived experiences of literacy and image work? If so, in what ways? How did they respond to the image work? Once the research ended, Terry and Jennifer sat together for a week to look across all of the data for recurrent themes, but, most important, for conceptual and theoretical motifs. They found Alecia Jackson and Lisa Mazzei's "plugged in" approach (2012, 2) to analysis—there needs to be some chaos, making and unmaking during data analysis—especially helpful to excavate findings, ideas, and concepts. For us, part of the chaos of analyzing data is plugging into theory, where production of knowledge involves "emerging as assemblage, creation from chaos" (Jackson and Mazzei 2012, 2). Although there is a danger in this kind of theorizing because it melds together divergent theories from separate traditions that have distinct lineages, what appealed to us about the "plugging in" approach is its openness and suppleness of thinking with theory.

SEEING THROUGH THE POSTHUMAN

Scholars across disciplines have acknowledged an overemphasis on humans as the starting point of research in contrast to taking an expansive—"posthuman"—view of the world as populated by both humans and nonhumans and thus a view attributing agency to the things, objects, and material worlds that surround us (Alaimo and Hekman 2008; Barad 2003; 2007; Kuby and Gutshall Rucker 2016). Two important aspects of the posthuman are that it brings to light what it means to be human (Braidotti 2013; Truman 2019) and that it also allows us as humans to decenter our gaze. In "Rolling in the Deep," we encouraged our research participants to turn away from "the human," to take in "the nonhuman," and to perceive the world differently— to turn their gaze away from their lives, addictions, and mental illness and to focus on materials and matter. Sometimes the materials were relational in nature—representing parts of themselves in photos— but, at other times, they were ways to unknow (Vasudevan 2011), undo, or defamiliarize themselves with their lives.

Although multimodal and multiliteracies scholars discuss materiality (Cope and Kalantzis 2000; Kress 1997; New London Group 1996), in this chapter, the focus is on what humans *do* to materials in literacy learning. A key difference here is that, taking a posthumanist approach, we examine how humans and materials become "intra-actively" entangled (Kuby and Rowsell 2017). Indeed, central to posthumanist research is a focus on human and nonhuman intra-actions (Hultman and Lenz Taguchi 2010), over and against a focus on language and words or on humans. Taking a relational materialist approach to sense making moves people away from reading the world through a human-centric lens to focus instead on the varied ways of knowing, engaging, and thinking through objects and materials. In other words, there is a mutual engagement that happens between materials, matter, humans, and nonhumans, as argued in the work of Karen Barad (2007), Donna Haraway (2008), and Elizabeth Grosz (2005). In "Rolling in the Deep," nonhuman objects like a glass window, black flowers, and a mannequin served as constitutive factors in how the group came to know and understand themselves and their relations with one another. Our study participants' photographs strongly illustrate how co-researchers engaged with eclectic and familiar objects.

From Barad (2007), we adopted the notion of "intra-activity." Whereas *inter*activity is human-centric, focusing on interpersonal relationships between people, *intra*-activity focuses on relationships between people and matter, or between "the human" and "the nonhuman," which are in a constant state of intra-activity with varying degrees of intensity. Taken on the third day of the research study, Emily's photographs (figures 2.1a and 2.1b) offer examples of how she was intra-active with materials and matter. During her interview (August 2016), she described how she was drawn to nonhuman, material worlds and talked about escaping into drawings, books, and nature: "I grew up in the woods, like, I do not like being in the city, it's not really something that appeases me. Umm, being here, and, like, being able to just, like, step out into a bunch of greenery not far from town is ideal for me. And it takes me out of myself." Here Emily connects her interior world with the exterior world—they stick and adhere within and around the blue paperweight (Ahmed 2014). Most of the time, Emily was either drawing and listening or sitting close by and chatting with the group. She talked about her hometown, nature, getting back to her roots, which she did, moving back to her hometown at the conclusion of the research study.

AFFECT AND PLACE: RESEARCH REFLECTIONS

"Rolling in the Deep" was filled with affect as well as with human and nonhuman expression. Although our participants' varied concerns and afflictions made us both feel stretched beyond our own knowledge base and experience, we agreed that the research taught us a lot about ourselves and our own weaknesses and strengths as researchers, and we most certainly saw things differently by the end of the project.

In addition, our research involved entanglements with moving bodies, materials, photographs, and some measure of spoken and written language. Bound within it was a more resonant belief in "unknowing" (Vasudevan 2011) and in a Russian artistic method called "defamiliarization" that prompts people to abandon familiar realities to reimagine things and events in a different, unfamiliar light. Defamiliarization was devised by Viktor Shklovsky (1917), who used it as an artistic technique to cast common things in an unfamiliar light. Such an approach to material engagements invites perceptual, embodied responses and the "revisioning" of places—seeing them in a new light.

Our process of analysis involved detailed field notes, visual artifacts, and poststudy interviews. Every three days, we had debriefing sessions with the research team. To illustrate the type of field notes we took, here are two instances, the first near the beginning and the second at the end of our research project:

Field notes for June 15, 2016—Rolling in the Deep: Seeing Differently (Photography—My First Day)

The first day of the research study and I feel a bit over my head. The Head of the Organization warned me about it when she said, "how much trauma can one person take?" And, that is what I saw on all of their faces today. First to my left sat Dexter, a 26-year-old young man, who does not fit in well or easily with the group and who generally seems marginalized. He moved to 9 different places as a child and he says, "I have no friends." He shares random bits of information about his childhood and tries to reach out to people. He gravitated to me from the start and sat next to me, but then moved around a bit ... Terry started with introductions and then moved onto her PowerPoint looking at different images and asking the group to guess what was in the photo—they saw a range of wild and imaginative things. They shared stories about their childhood. The group responded well to the discussion and to the sharing circle.

Field notes for July 20, 2016—Rolling in the Deep: Seeing Differently (Movement—My Last Day)

Today was the last day and I felt so emotional. This group has really got under my skin. They are smart and kind and thoughtful. They do movement work in such a natural way that it amazes me. They are the most unpredictable group I have ever worked with. But they are probably one of the most creative groups, too. Glenys has everyone move and feel (relatively) at ease with it. I like watching them move and there are some gifted people in the group—Emily, Matt, Greg, and Maya exhibited real joy in the process. I know that the project did not work for everyone, but it certainly worked for most.

Most of the field notes consider images taken by participants that were unique in style and composition and that reflected the idiosyncratic nature of the group. Angelo liked to take photographs of signs, close-up shots of parking meters, and angled shots of architecture. Greg took photographs of feet and street detritus. Because Maya had lymphedema in her legs and was in her wheelchair most of the time, many of her photographs were about immobility, depicting people in wheelchairs or with canes. Maya has transformed since the project: she has returned to her own art after a very long hiatus, has hosted three different art exhibits in St. Catharines, and she is back to writing plays. She no longer uses either a wheelchair or a cane, and she has lost significant weight.

Not all of the "Rolling in the Deep" stories are as promising and happy. One of the most enthusiastic young men in the project, who exhibited a tremendous capacity for acting and movement, died of an overdose a year after the project ended. To get a sense of all of the "Rolling in the Deep" participants, please see table 2.1.

Table 2.1. "Rolling in the Deep" participants

Pseudonym	Personal history
Amir	Age: 60 (but 18 at heart). Born in Pakistan; came to Canada in 2003. Successful consultant in Pakistan (owned his own company). Never married; no children.
Angelo	Age: 42. Born in the Niagara region. Has worked at Walmart and in a factory.
Carley	Age: 40. Born in Nova Scotia but family moved to Niagara area when she was a baby. Has college degree and 23-year-old daughter.
Dexter	Age: 26. Born in Niagara region. Raised by single mother and often moved around region as child.
Emily	Age: 30. Born in Peterborough, Ontario. Though she described herself as a "career" drug addict, she is in recovery and on a good path now.
Greg	Age: 36. Born and raised in Niagara region. Never married; no children. High school diploma, went to college but did not finish and enjoyed project.
Margaret	Age: 59. Born and raised in Niagara region. Three children—two daughters from her first marriage; son from her second marriage. Was photographer before project and is happy to be one again.
Matt	Age unknown (did not want to disclose). Born and raised in Niagara region.
Maya	Age: around 60. Born in United States and moved to Niagara area with her family in 1965 (parents are Canadian; brother would have been drafted for Vietnam War and parents wanted to avoid that). Was artist and playwright for many years in Montreal before joining project.
Stephen	Age: 39 Born in Kitchener/Waterloo and raised in Cambridge, Ontario; moved to Niagara area in 2000 with his family. Never married; no children.
Todd	Age: 26. Born in Nigeria. Came to Canada in 2014 and hopes to be a musician.

PUSHING AGAINST HISTORIES AND THINKING ABOUT PLACE AS ETHNOGRAPHIC KNOWLEDGE

A key dimension of ethnographic fieldwork entails becoming attuned to and constituted in ethnographic sites (Heath and Street with Mills 2008). Research studies profiled in *Living Literacies* aspired to learn in and as a part of the contexts in which the studies took place. Places like Rotherham and St. Catharines are at the heart of the book; they carry with them not only material things such as people, locations, hubs, community artifacts, monuments, and institutions, but also immaterial things such as histories, associations, emotions, and memories.

In "Rolling in the Deep," besides drawing on and pushing against histories and associations, we (Terry and Jennifer) also adopted Sarah Pink's method (2006) of ethnographic research. Pink approaches data collection as a felt, sensed experience of place—walking through streets, looking at visuals in store windows, at trees and hills within the surrounding landscape. We concentrated strongly on this kind of emplaced inquiry, where study participants would walk with camera in hand around the neighborhood of the Niagara Arts Sudio, taking photos of street signs, alleyways, even close-ups of cobwebs. Feelings, senses, and experiences seeped into their photos not only in the ways these were shot, but also in the ways they were visually composed. Terry worked closely with participants like Amir, who at first struggled with the whole point of taking close-ups of material objects. But when she taught him how to telescope into fractals as patterns, it appealed to his architectural background, and he found the process intriguing, even enlightening—shifting from cynicism to curiosity when he looked closely at a spiderweb, for instance.

Focusing on material worlds, Sarah Pink (2009) helpfully pushes multimodal ethnographers to take more account of the felt, sensory nature of multimodal work, and we saw this enacted during "Rolling in the Deep." Pink and Kerstin Leder Mackley (2014, 146) talk about the need to be "in there" and "part of the flow of everyday life" when conducting ethnographic research. Because our participants focused on everyday and displayed objects, they were able to capture their color, shape, heft, size, position, lightness, and darkness. It is difficult to separate out the material aspects of objects from how the objects make people feel (Pahl and Rowsell 2010). "Rolling in the Deep" participants articulated this difficulty when they described how interconnected their senses were and how hard it was for them to differentiate sensory and felt qualities from material aspects of the objects they photographed. By contrast, the forms of literacy they faced daily—on job applications, legal documents, and so on—were more autonomous and regulatory and based on words. They spoke of words as being associated with authority, and they generally preferred a more interconnected and relational—a more lived—approach to literacy learning. It is for this reason that the photography unit of the research study was particularly rewarding for them because it drew naturally on the ways that materials and objects interfaced with senses.

THEORIZING AFFECT AND EMOTION: SEEING AS A STICKY EMOTION

Sara Ahmed (2014) writes about emotion, bodily sensations, and individuals. She speaks of an "aboutness" of emotions that implies a way of apprehending the world. Emotions are about and shaped by objects—both human and nonhuman. Since histories are in place before someone encounters a human or nonhuman object, emotions and feelings are not *in* the object. Ahmed (2014, 26) analyzes what she calls "the sociality of objects"—that is, how objects impress themselves on and "stick" to people. In other words, feelings, emotions, and affect do not reside *in* objects, but they circulate around people and they can stick to them. Or, as Ahmed (2014, 10) puts it: "Feelings become a form of social presence rather than self-presence." She concentrates on the production and circulation of emotion and "the sticking of signs to bodies" (Ahmed 2014, 14). To examine closely how emotions are produced, Ahmed (2014, 13) focuses on the question of *what* sticks: "I suggest that the work of emotion involves the 'sticking' of signs to bodies: for example, when others become 'hateful,' then actions of 'hate' are directed against them." She tracks how words for feelings or objects for feelings generate, circulate, and "stick" to people. The doing of emotions is inextricably linked with the relations between signs and bodies. From pain to hate to fear to disgust to love, Ahmed listens to the affective life of moments in time, extracting the "stickiness" as a production of emotions.

In what resonates strongly with Ahmed's conceptual framing of emotion, experiencing and knowing were the ways our research group was affected by things. Thinking about the close-up image of a blue paperweight (figure 2.1a) that Emily took illustrates how objects carry agency for people that revive and bring forth emotions and feelings (Pahl and Rowsell 2010). Emily has suffered from addiction since she was twelve years old. In and out of rehabilitation for years, she is now in recovery, free from addiction and social anxiety, and wants to be an addiction counselor. The paperweight sits on her desk in her apartment, and she will frequently look through it as a part of a daily rite. When she holds the paperweight to the light, Emily sees it as a portal to somewhere else. Actively photographing it and journaling about it have given her a reflective space to think about how it has steadied her.

Ahmed (2014) does not engage as much with visuals as she does with in-the-moment intra-actions between people and signs. Here the image is the starting point—generating "stickiness." We argue in this chapter that research participants' engagements with objects produced forms of stickiness that ranged across the emotions of fear, loneliness, and hope and that were accessed through engagements with objects as analyzed in the next section. Every moment is vital and profound in its potential to make a difference across multiple scales of space and time (Lemke 2000), to "mark bodies," and to "linger on the skin." Or, as Ahmed (2006, 8–9) explains:

> Orientations, then, are about the intimacy of bodies and their dwelling places.... Bodies may become orientated in this responsiveness to the world around them.... In turn, given the histories of such responses, which accumulate as impressions on the skin, bodies do not dwell in spaces that are exterior but rather are shaped by their dwellings and take shape by dwelling.

Rather than focusing on bodies and people, we opted for an eclectic mix of objects, signage, and familiar artifacts. There was a mindful feel to the exercise of photographing objects that the research group frequently called "getting out of our heads for two hours and not thinking about addiction."

ILLUSTRATING SEEING AS A LIVED LITERACY

Although the emotional "stickiness" that happened within the research group was, for the most part, positive and bonding, at times, it gave rise to tension, anger, and certainly sadness. "Rolling in the Deep" was an emotionally charged research study, and emotions were etched into the participants' photographs.

GREG: GETTING OUT OF MY HEAD

Greg usually arrived in bare feet, wearing a tie and seersucker shorts, often dancing into the study space and jumping up and down, with his fingers raised in a peace sign. There was a lightness and levity to Greg that we so appreciated throughout the research.

Greg would freely admit to using meth regularly. He developed the closest bond with Emily, although he got along with everyone. What he loved most about the photography was "getting out of my head and just shooting" streetscapes:

> As much as I've never really done photography so I am just trying to take a lot of pictures, and I want to see what comes out groovy. I figure as much as like when I do art I just kind of throw it all down on paper too and don't think about it and then when it comes out its groovy right? So I try not to think when I do this shit. (August 2016)

Greg's photography often had to do with the grittier side of street life and included, for example, graphic close-ups of feet. His pictures are unashamedly honest, stark, and usually close-up. Figure 2.2 shows a series of close-up shots of feet he took as a collage to represent his everyday. Walking barefoot in his community connected him strongly to the land and to his home. He often shared how much he enjoyed living street life and sleeping out in nature. When he was not living in an apartment or sleeping on someone's sofa, he often lived and slept outside in a tent. Thinking about Pink's work (2009)—place as experiential—is an ideal way to analyze how Greg intra-acted with photographs and the visual. Greg and the objects that populate his images display a range of emotions depending on his mood. Although, at times, they exhibit sadness and despair, much of the time, his images are playful, silly, even joyful. There is something in Greg's images that captures a grittier, lived side of life that, at first, feels uncomfortable, but once you look closer, and talk more with him, you soon realize that Greg does not believe in patterns and strict rules and defies them, by, for example, not wearing shoes but wearing formal trousers and a tie.

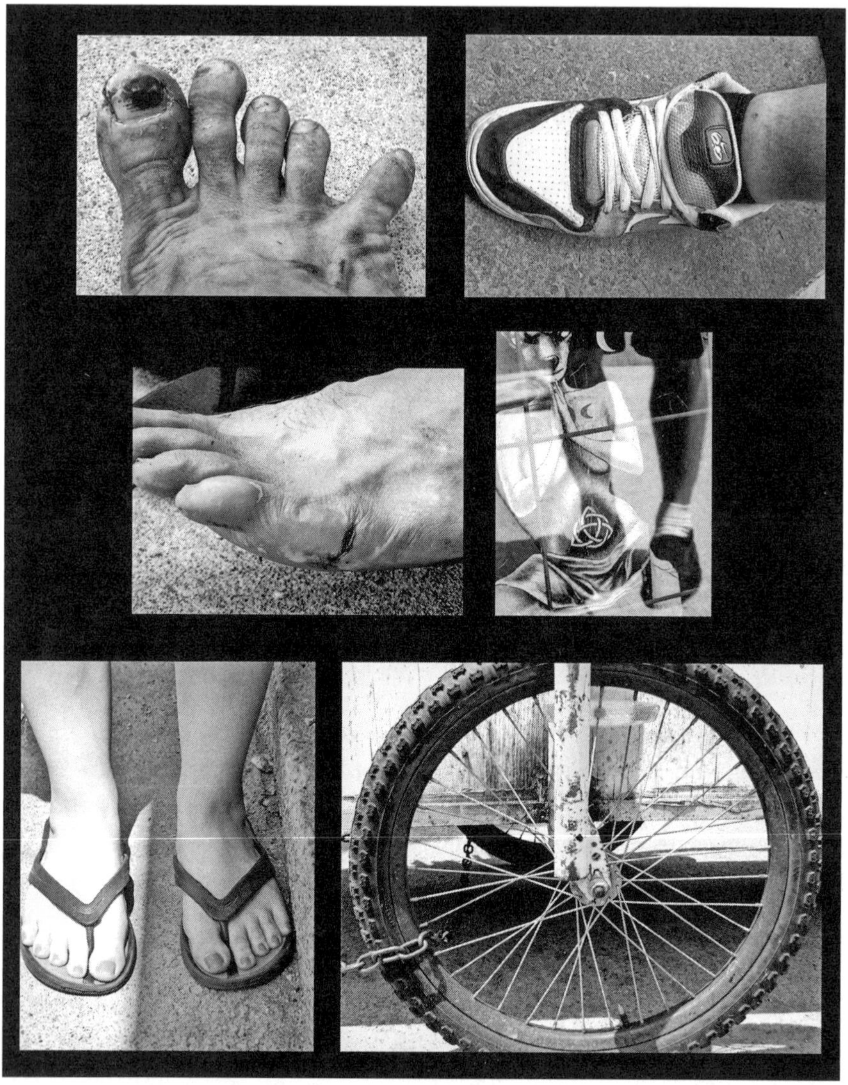

Figure 2.2
"A Collage of Feet" by Greg

CARLEY: DRAWING CENTERS ME

At the beginning of the research study, Carley sat on the edge of the group looking shy and hesitant. In the first few days, she could be seen hunched over her pad, drawing circular and geometric designs. When she drew, she was engrossed and told Jennifer that drawing centered her. But her love of doodling and drawing did not always translate into her photography. She liked taking photos, but she would return to her drawings and even took a series of photographs of them, as seen in figure 2.3.

Asked about art during her interview (August 2016), Carley told us:

> I got the inspiration for art from the hospital outpatient groups, one of the earlier ones was called "Journey to Recovery," um, they suggested it, and they had a lot of those Zen doodle books around, and they would let us take pages out, and that was when I realized that I liked doing the art, but I didn't like the Zen doodles, so I started trying my own, and that was how it developed into my own work. I had done some when I had stayed at the Y for a while, probably, like, in 2002, I had done a little bit like that, but I didn't really explore too much. But it was the same kind of style of work. That was mostly, like, the past few months, like, eight months probably.

Figure 2.3
"Doodling" by Carley

Carley described herself as "a scanner," always observing people around her and trying to protect herself. She admitted in the interview that she did not do much scanning during the research study. Her drawings display what Tim Ingold (2013, 95) describes as "materials flowing and leaking through agency." For Carley, doodling had a kind of material agency: she could locate the kind of mood she was experiencing within each doodle she drew.

Carley thinks through her drawings—"as the artisan thinks *from* materials" (Ingold 2013, 94). Emotionally, Carley felt safer on her own, and doing artwork in social environments often made her feel unprotected, even isolated. As she said in her interview: "It is really hard for someone who has trust issues to be in a group, so it was a huge accomplishment to work with the 'Rolling' participants for sure." Over the course of the study, Carley moved from outside the circle to become one of the central figures in the group. Carley and Jennifer felt the closest bond during the research; they frequently sat beside or near each other and would take photos or do movement work together. Carley found co-researching and living through the visual to be a slow, though steady process, but, in the end, she felt right at home in "Rolling in the Deep."

MARGARET: LOOKING AT THINGS DIFFERENTLY

With a smile that lit up the room, Margaret sat in the center of the "Rolling" group as a calming presence for everyone. She seemed to take to the research almost immediately, sitting with people, talking about how close-ups of everyday sites made her see things "from a totally different perspective," like the black flowers she passed by every day but did not give a second thought to. She described the intricacy of downtown architecture, but she was most inspired by seeing everyday things in her life in an entirely new way. Although she had been a professional photographer, she had never appreciated how experimenting with angles, perspectives, and lighting makes things look so different. Also, she loved the idea of Terry's "story fractals."

In her interview (August 2016), Margaret talked about her former life: "I was a photographer before with, uh, film, and this was the first time with a digital camera, so I was, like, 'Wow, this is great!' I could snap pictures of anything, and hundreds of pictures in a day of things that I see."

Figure 2.4
"Renewal and Rebirth" by Margaret

What was novel to Margaret was the notion of looking closely at material worlds and, in a posthuman sense, giving them agency and life. Drawn to the idea that material worlds can tell stories, Margaret would connect her photos with an idea like hope or renewal, as seen in figure 2.4. In doing so, she became what Ingold (2013, 25) describes as a wayfarer "whose task is to enter the grain of the world's becoming and bend it to an evolving purpose."

MAYA: I LIKED BEING AMONG PEOPLE

Like Carley, Maya tended to sit behind others in the group or on the side of the room. She looked like someone who had lots of stories to tell if only she chose to share them. She rode in on a wheelchair, which she left outside, and walked with a cane. What Maya liked most about the research was observing the group and watching how others made meaning. She had been an accomplished artist and playwright, though she did not speak much about her past. But, then, during her interview (August 2016), she decided to tell us about her coming out:

> You see, back in those days you couldn't come out. It was like the worst possible thing you could be, in, like to be called queer, that's what they used to call you back then, "queer," and it wasn't reclaimed yet, you know—the word wasn't reclaimed yet. It was like the worst thing you could be. Everybody made fun of it. So I didn't even acknowledge that I was gay until much later.

Her photos have a rawness about them, such as images of a prostitute with her breasts showing, candid shots of older people in wheelchairs, or dirty alleyways. But the most recurrent images are of immobility—of confinement, whether to wheelchairs or to beds.

Maya deliberately gave a graininess to the photo in figure 2.5 to both blur the woman's identity and to cast a haze over her life. There is a sense of invisibility to people in her photos. Indeed, Maya's photographs exhibit an emotional stickiness in Ahmed's sense of the entanglement of bodies, objects, and histories: "Stickiness is the effect of the histories

Figure 2.5
"Wheeling across the Street" by Maya

of contact between bodies, objects, and signs" (Ahmed 2014, 90). Her haunting images uncover deeper feelings about life and the sense of isolation she increasingly opened up about over the course of the research. After the study ended, the director of the support center found a space for Maya to paint. She has since hosted small exhibits in St. Catharines; she has started writing plays again and is in much better health.

TODD: YOU HAVE TO BE PATIENT

One of the younger participants, Todd moved from Nigeria to Germany, then to Canada. Like Greg, he struggled with addiction, which seemed to grow worse over the course of the research, a development the team connected with outside events that took place during the study. He enjoyed some of the sessions, but, even though he showed a good eye for photography, it was hard for him to stay focused. An aspiring musician, Todd spoke a great deal about what he was composing and the types of music he loved. He felt that his composing brought out the best in him:

> Yeah, it help me to see my creative side and I did a piece called ... and it just helped me to put light into the how big my ideas and little how no matter how miniscule or how little it is there is still something there that could come out big through art and I don't know, I know in the future when I get to better levels and more programs like this come up we can learn, I can still learn more and be better every day. Every day I am still learning. I am hoping to learn and I will be a better person in the end of the day, so that is just it. (October 2016)

Todd talked about being patient for things to happen. In his photographs, he focused on textures and colors. He liked bold colors, which made him think about his African roots. He often took close-ups of colorful objects, whose angles, shapes, and textures caught his eye, as the triptych of his work in figure 2.6 illustrates.

LIVING LITERACIES AS PART OF HUMAN LIFE

In "Rolling in the Deep," the camera gave group members a screen between themselves and the rest of the world. Objects that participants visualized sometimes provoked their thoughts; at other times, the objects simply got them out of their heads and away from their addictions. The key "Rolling in the Deep" finding in relation to living literacies is that the

Figure 2.6
Todd's triptych

participants recognized that their everyday counts as an important forum for meaning making and that they can reimagine their everyday through art. During those warm summer afternoons, it felt as if the camera gave them all a new start or fresh look at their community.

Respecting literacy practices that are real and part of the everyday—and that acknowledge the richness and complexity of literacy—grounds literacy in people's lives. Greg reflected on living literacy in his community:

> I've been hanging around more, like, the people at the lower spectrum of poverty and social stature. So those are the people that I like to try to be with, talk with, learn from. My friends. So profs don't usually need my help. As much as, like, I don't try, what am I? Hmmm, I try not to make assumptions or label people as this or that, so in any situation as much as I have experienced people and that helps me to understand mostly how they relate to situations or kind of what they are after, or what their desires are, because we do things for personal reasons, right? So I always see their potential based on what I have experienced from them. And I try not to label them and always hope for the best, you know.

Trust in the mercy of the universe. Hope for the best situations, good experiences with good intentions. (Greg, October 2016)

In this chapter, we have presented a research study that spurred its eleven photograph-taking participants to see both what *is* and what *could be* in their everyday (more on "What if ... ?" and "could be" approaches in chapter 4, "Hoping"). And we have shown how a living literacies approach is threaded between and across these participants' photography, living both within the stuff of their photographs and within their stories—and creating a tapestry of material and human encounters tied in with affective and nonhuman elements.

Figure 3.1
"End Racism" by Shaheen Shah

3

DISRUPTING: THE LITERACIES OF ACTIVISM

Kate Pahl and Zanib Rasool

An artist's own experience is central to the artwork.
—Shaheen Shah (2018, 57)

A living literacies approach to research attends to the process of doing the research. Much of the research described in this book is dialogic and speaks with many voices. It is constructed in between sites and spaces. Doing living literacies research is relational and can be disruptive, angry, complex, and multivoiced—like the sites where the research takes place. Here we enact living literacies through a multivoiced chapter, written as a dialogue between two people who have worked together for some time. Zanib is a scholar and activist who has served for many years as a community development worker in Rotherham, a Yorkshire town in the north of England. She has been a researcher on a number of research projects including the "Imagine" and the "Taking Yourselves Seriously" studies (see "Chapter 6 Featured Studies" in appendix). These research studies drew on coproduction as a methodology to consider how arts-based methodologies could lead to a better understanding of community engagement and cohesion (Rasool 2017). Kate is an academic who has worked within communities for many years to highlight the everyday lived experience, the "common cultures," that can be found within them (Pahl 2014a). Our research incorporates working with artists, poets, and writers to make sense of lived experiences within communities through artistic methodologies.

This chapter is about Kate's and Zanib's lived experience and weaves this into a discussion of the literacies of activism. Kate brings her experience of working with Zanib over many years to explore together the nature of community literacies, with a particular focus on South Asian stories and objects (Pahl and Rowsell 2010). In working together, we have come to recognize how different kinds of knowledge are braided together in particular ways. Though we both share a commitment to community development, given our different vantage points, we thought it best for our chapter to move in and out of each of our voices in a back-and-forth exchange as we take turns to reflect on the research it presents.

WHAT DOES IT MEAN TO DISRUPT?

Artistic methodologies provide a way in to a living literacies approach in that they draw on embodied and tacit ways of knowing, feeling their way into the world (Ravetz and Ravetz 2016). Artists can highlight lived experience in ways that can shock or surprise us. For example, the image in figure 3.1 by Rotherham artist Shaheen Shah (who publishes under the name "Shahin Shah") reflects her experience of racism as a young girl: "This image tries to articulate the fear resulting from racist attacks and how they manifest in many different forms—it may be words, actions, the instigation of animals, or isolation" (Shah 2018, 56). Shah's artwork describes and brings to light her lived experience as a British Asian girl growing up in a small town in the United Kingdom and suffering the effects of racism. She argues that "South Asian artists … are best placed to tell stories of our heritage.… There has to be an emotional link to those stories—those stories are reminders of our heritage, as we negotiate new roots in other parts of the world" (Shah 2018, 57). Shah's focus on lived experienced has an activist edge—it brings viewers and readers into the emotional experience of the artist.

Kate is conscious that much of her knowledge rests on white privilege, having been brought up as a middle-class white woman who went to an elite university (see Reddo-Lodge 2017). She studied English literature and draws on literary sources as well as sociological research to make sense of communities' stories. Zanib's story is more complex, and her road to university was longer. Born in Newcastle upon Tyne to immigrant parents the same year as Kate, Zanib gained her degree in midlife and is now working on a doctorate. In her work, she has drawn on the knowledge production practices of Maori scholarship and critical race theory (Ladson-Billings and Tate 1995; Mahuika 2008). Zanib's knowledge is community based and provides a cultural insider's ("emic") perspective on everyday hidden community literacy practices. Despite our differences, however, we share a history of community development work and a passion for racial equality. In our coedited book *Re-imagining Contested Communities* (Campbell et al. 2018), we expanded on the complexities of cowriting across different spaces and learning from each other in the process of doing so. Writing together has been a privilege, but power differences between us continue to affect the work we produce. The university Kate previously worked at was unaware of Zanib's strong contribution to the "Imagine" project. As a doctoral student, Zanib was positioned in a particular way. Kate held more power as a professor at that institution. Articulating and making transparent this process is important. Michel Foucault (1980, 52) argues that power cannot be exercised without knowledge: "It is impossible for knowledge not to engender power, since knowledge produces power."

A living literacies approach attends to the production of knowledge (see chapter 1). The literacies of dissent are inherently dialogic, creative, and disruptive; indeed, they are rooted in a disruptive approach to the production of knowledge. Ideas that can help with understanding this include the concept of "agonism," from Chantal Mouffe (2007), who argued:

> According to the agonistic approach, critical art is art that foments dissensus, that makes visible what the dominant consensus tends to obscure and obliterate. It is constituted by a manifold of artistic practices aiming at giving a voice to all those who are silenced within the framework of the existing hegemony.

This perspective highlights the need, as a priority, to give voice to those who are silenced within the "dominant consensus." The idea of "dissensus," from Jacques Rancière (2010), can enable an understanding of art as a space of difference, a rupture in the settled norms of everyday life. The research we have done together has explored how creative arts, poetry, and visual arts, can offer a space to articulate different ideas and to construct activist narratives. This leads to questions such as "Whose voices count in collaborations and why?," "What kinds of voices do artistic modes of enquiry let in?," and "How do we incorporate diverse voices in research?" (Campbell et al. 2018, 205)

We echo the words of Courtney Hanny and colleagues (2018, 47): "In order to work against what might be seen as complacency on the part of isolated universities, and to foster the spirit of authentic partnership, hierarchies have to be challenged, and extant assumptions about *whose knowledge counts* need to be deconstructed" (italics in original). Coauthoring, they argue, "is a practice of challenging epistemic injustice" (Hanny et al. 20198, 46). The work then becomes a process of excavating and recognizing the different voices within the writing. The literacies of activism are collaborative, which produces accounts of literacy research that are rooted in questions of voice, power, and diversity and who gets to tell the story.

In order to present these ideas, we have situated our work within vignettes of practice, drawn from different projects over the years, projects that raise issues of voice and representation in the literacies of activism and that explore the uncomfortable nature of activist voices. A reflective piece by Zanib describes her experience of racism through writing and poetry. We also explore the practice of collaboration (see Rasool 2017), which highlights the importance of listening, voice, and reclaiming history in an activist literacies approach. The writing of those taking such an approach is divergent, reflecting a dialogic mode of thinking (Bakhtin 1981) in which the ideas inherent in the approach—agonism, dissensus, divergence, and dialogue (see glossary)—are brought alive.

Working together in this way involves attention to ways of knowing that might be called "local" but that can bridge the local and the global in a shared engagement with social change and transformation (Blackburn and Clark 2007). And it involves a commitment to rethink ways of knowing in communities by viewing them from the perspectives of indigenous scholars (Tuhiwai Smith, Tuck, and Yang 2019). These perspectives help us to rethink what it is to do research within everyday settings—and to reflect about whose voices are being heard and where.

Sara Ahmed (2017, 102) calls for the need to "theorize from our own embodied work" and also to be attentive to the politics of citation trails and what they mean. As two white scholars, Jennifer and Kate have been aware of the gaps, collusions, and deficiencies of their own worldview, and have sought to undo or decenter their own epistemological standpoints in the cowriting of these chapters. For our part, having worked with each other for more than ten years, we have cowritten this chapter as a dialogue that instantiates this idea. But, as George Moses and colleagues (2018, ix) remind us: "The work of dialogue across difference is difficult work." Sometimes our writing converges; sometimes it diverges. Our voices do not always sit together—Zanib is a black woman and Kate is a white woman. Although we have learned to listen to each other and trust each other in our shared work, we do not always carry the same ideas or write with the same voice. Our writing is fractured by race and class. Kate has had to recognize her more privileged role in this process. Our work together is threaded through with voices of young people. We share a passion for libraries, literature, and reading poetry. Zanib writes poetry, and her own poetic voice enlivens these pages. Together, in our discussions, we consider how artistic methodologies prompt new ways of understanding living literacies to argue, persuade, dissent, and disrupt.

In this chapter, we focus on the voices of girls and young women, who are commonly excluded from discourses of power. Considering the politics of knowledge production helps us recognize the ways in which white oppression has excluded black discourses as "other" (see Reddo-Lodge 2017). It provides an expanded methodology for addressing the literacies of activism, in particular the "uncomfortable literacies" that refuse to conform. And though the process of bringing different intertextual references together in the "dark cave" of making is complex and contested (Bhabha 2009), doing so can create something new. A way of articulating this process is through the literacies of dissent, as these are expressed through art and within an ethical space (Rancière 2010).

Zanib's poem "The Bus Ride Home" (below) is a visceral and powerful account of the lived experience of racism. Writing against racism begins a process of refusal that brings everyday experience into an artistic mode, in this case, poetry. The everyday can also become a key site for the literacies of activism. Zanib describes how women gathering together by the school gates can be understood as a form of collective action—an acknowledgment of the need to find the "commons" in public spaces (Gilbert 2014). Activist literacies place an emphasis on radical hope that can resist the dominant discourses of neoliberalism and capitalism that tend to drive identity politics. Through small, incremental change (Hamdi 2004) and a stubborn refusal to give in to more powerful voices, transformational change can happen.

The literacies of activism can be enacted through silence. Many young people do not want to employ particular modes of representation such as film and visual images (Pahl 2019). They might not have access to digital resources or free Internet access. The literacies of resistance can involve silence, embodiment, feeling, and nonrepresentational forms of expression (Truman 2019). The resonance of these activities can cross generations and can include embodied and artistic methodologies. Not all young people have the capacity to become involved in organized resistance (Jenson, Dahya, and Fisher 2014, 2). Many find themselves overwhelmed by the struggle to live a life within conditions of poverty in barely habitable neighborhoods. Indeed, just "living your life" is enough of a struggle in many postindustrial communities where the state has withdrawn support and employment opportunities remain few (Pahl and Pool 2011). Although some kinds of youth resistance are mobilized through interaction with community media projects, Chelsey Hauge (2014) argues that these activities might not be congruent with the lived experiences of young people. And Jennifer Jenson, Negin Dahya, and Stephanie Fisher (2014, 2) argue that the young people in the neighborhoods they were researching had already experienced subjugation:

> Power relations determine whose voices are heard, and for young people in our study, they are excluded from most of the decision-making processes that pertain to them and are subject to adult authority. Moreover, these students live in a neighborhood whose positive attributes are rarely celebrated or recognized city wide.

Young people might refuse to work within the spaces constructed for them—or they might reconstruct them anew. Sarah Truman (2019, 111) writes how "refusal, re-storying and the capaciousness of affect have the potential [to] rewrite dominant orders of knowledge." Her exploration of a young woman's refusal to write a poem enacted what it was like to be a young Muslim woman whose voice was not heard within mainstream cultural spaces. Negin Dahya (2017) has highlighted the complexity of the idea of voice, recognizing that it is important to question "unproblematic" representations of students' voices. The politics of knowledge production and the practices that surround this process need highlighting across community and education settings.

KATE AND ZANIB: MAKING THE DIALOGUE COME ALIVE

The dialogue between us illustrates the nature of activist literacies. Our discussion reveals how these literacies are made through dialogue, when people converse through inhabiting difficult, sometimes uncomfortable spaces.

UNCOMFORTABLE LITERACIES: FEELING "NOTHING" TO THE GOVERNMENT

Kate writes: The literacies of activism can feel uncomfortable. Many of the stories in this chapter are hard to read ("The Bloody Boots," "The Bus Ride Home"). Adults can feel threatened by young people questioning them, developing ideas that do not "fit" with how they think they should behave. This, in effect, unsettles their views of what literacy is supposed to be, offering instead what it *could be*—a mode of resistance and dissenting voices.

The image in figure 3.2 illustrates an example of activist literacies. In 2013, together with an artist, Steve Pool, and a youth worker, Marcus Hurcombe, I worked with a group of young people (aged 14 to 24) who came to a youth center in Rotherham to coproduce a film about young

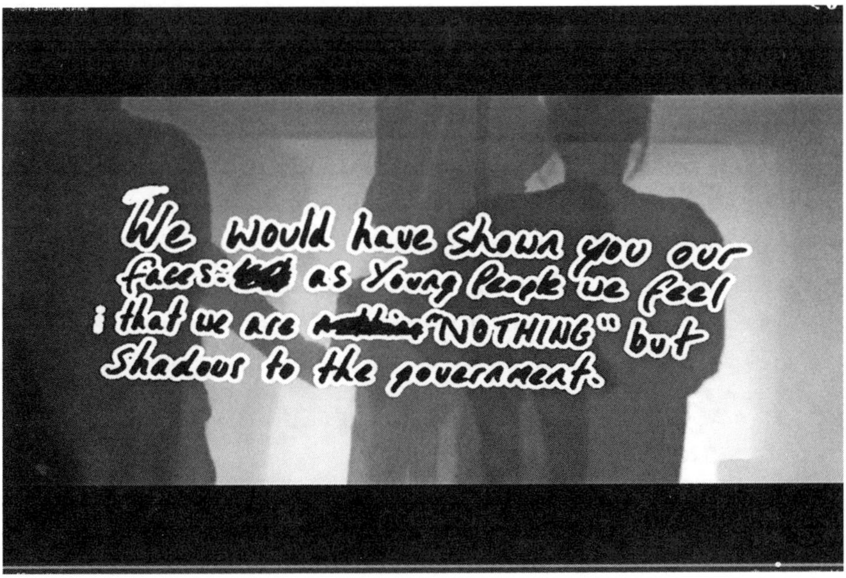

Figure 3.2
Still from film co-created by young people, with inscribed slogan

people's relationship to government. The film was part of an Arts and Humanities Research Council–funded study called "Making Meaning Differently" (see "Chapter 3 Featured Studies" in appendix) and was commissioned by the UK civil service to find out about how young people relate to the idea of governance and local government structures. Our participants met as a group and discussed the ways in which they did not feel safe and did not feel listened to, after which they scripted a play about this experience. They also danced to music and wrote comments about their feelings, which were added to the film to press their message home. The image in figure 3.2 is of one such still from the film they made, using dance, slogans, and shadow puppets, that told a story of going to the police for help and not being heard (Pool and Pahl 2015).

The message that the young people gave was hard for some adults to hear—Steve and I presented it to a group of policy makers, who later reflected on the format of the film being somewhat different from what they were used to (Connelly et al. 2015). This kind of message is called an "uncomfortable literacy"—a way of resisting the "scripts" imposed on young people that tell them they can be safely ignored. Here, resistance is a form of multimodal articulation presented as a challenge. One of the concerns of those taking an activist literacies approach is that "uncomfortable" messages are much easier for some adults to hear when communicated in certain ways than in others. Thus, for example, mainstream government officials tend to consider messages conveyed in writing much easier to hear than those conveyed in visual and multimodal forms. That traditional school literacy practices have much greater sway than visual and multimodal communicational practices poses a challenge to literacy educators resisting a skills-based approach who might want to develop a wider repertoire of literacy practices, ones better able to articulate young people's concerns and feelings.

POETRY AS A FORM OF ACTIVISM: FEELING "STOOD ON REPEATEDLY"

Lily by Hafsah Wahid

I was yanked away from my family and friends
My petals were pulled painfully away from me
I have now been left in the dark to be stood on repeatedly

Zanib writes: I had been working with a small group of young women of South Asian heritage. We had the opportunity to write poems with the poet Helen Mort. This project aimed to explore young women's identities and hopeful visions of the future using poetry. Helen and I had booked a venue in a nearby youth center and planned to meet every Saturday. The first Saturday morning of the study, the group got locked out of the venue and decided to go to Clifton Park in the small town of Rotherham, near Sheffield. We found ourselves near the old bandstand. One of the young women, Hafsah Wahid (now aged 19), looked at a crushed lily lying by the bandstand and wrote the poem above—a poem that serves to reframe both the concept of "living literacies" and our links to the inside and the outside worlds we inhabit. Here we can understand how the lily and the young poet are entwined, how Hafsah is voicing her dissent at being pulled this way and that way between two cultures. The poem also resonates with me: as a Muslim black woman, I sometimes feel like I am constantly being stamped on and left bruised. In her writing on feminist theory, bell hooks (1984, 16) argues: "It is essential for continued feminist struggle that black women recognize their special vantage point our marginality gives us." The poems our young study participants wrote show how poetic forms can channel young people's complex emotions and provide a means of exploring identities that are fragile and fragmented, but also angry and coherent. Women on the periphery find poetry can empower them to fight back and can offer a counternarrative for their oppression in a world that "others" them.

Hafsah's poem also reminded me of the importance of public spaces for young people to meet. Parks can become creative places that bring diverse communities together. I can still sometimes remember hearing the colliery brass band play on sunny Sunday afternoons in Rotherham, when people from all backgrounds took their children to the park, and we were oblivious to our differences. The recent *Integrated Communities Strategy Green Paper* from the UK Ministry of Communities, Housing and Local Government (MHCLG 2018) calls for making better use of shared community spaces such as parks and libraries. We need to create safe parks for children once again. Clifton Park in Rotherham has activities going on year round that bring families out. Being reminded of myself as a child growing up in Rotherham led me to apply for funding to have a young people's event this year, called "Rotherham Rocks," showcasing young people's musical talents and taking over the bandstand once again.

LIBRARY LITERACIES: "WHY DON'T YOU SHOW PEOPLE RESPECT?"

Kate writes: Young people can unsettle the way we understand literacy. I realized this through a project called "Research Rebels" (see appendix) at a small community library in Rotherham, where a group of children regularly met. Although a librarian from a nearby library had said the children were "running riot" (Pahl and Allan 2011, 196), and others had suggested that the librarians there were simply unable to deal with them, when co-researcher Chloe Allan and I arrived on the scene, we saw a different picture. The librarians were committed to working with the children, some of whom came in to experience the warmth and friendliness of the library, have hot chocolate, and spend time together. Chloe and I decided to talk to them and ask if they would like to join our research study. Here Chloe describes our first encounter:

> The two teenage girls came in as Kate was explaining the challenge. When asked what questions they would ask for their research they all came up with some really good questions, which showed they had been following what we were doing and understood what was being asked. One of the main things which came up with the 3 older girls that were in the room was "Why do people mess about?' "Why don't people respect?' (Chloe Allan, field notes, March 22, 2010)

The three girls then went off to interview library users. But when they asked, "Why don't you show more respect?" this upset some of the users and caused some concern among the grown-ups:

> The teenage girls came back in with their "Flip" cameras and sat down. They talked a bit about what people had said. They said that some people had been rude and swore a lot when they interviewed them. They were surprised by a man [who swore] as they thought he was going to say he came in to use the computers. (Chloe Allan, field notes, March 22, 2010)

The self-named "Research Rebels" wanted change in their library. They turned their camera footage into a film that described the different responses to their questions about what the library meant to the people there, and that was shown to the Head of Libraries. The film raised troubling questions of who was respected within the library and why. And it turned on its head the idea of young people being the problem by asking, "Who has become the problem here?" Many writers have commented on how girls, and particularly working-class girls, are often seen as "the problem" (e.g., Jones 2006). The young people wanted to engage with making their library a better place; they asked for more drama and arts activities there. Often seen as difficult or even as "running riot" when they talked or made loud noises, their clearly audible presence in the library challenged the perception that libraries should be silent spaces. The vibrant, sometimes messy methods of our research project in documenting multiple literacies sometimes went against what some people thought libraries were for. Undaunted, however, the young people went about creating spaces for craft clubs and shared activities; their library became a space for "public pedagogies"—connecting classroom with real-life learning (see glossary)—one where creative activities burgeoned (see Hickey-Moody 2013). One of the fast-eroding rights young people have is the right to safe public spaces where they can meet and come together; they have very few such places. Drawing on the work of Edward Soja (2010) to look at young people's literacies from a "spatial justice" perspective, Joanne Larson (2014, 28) asks: "What does it mean to fight for the right to the city?" In the "Research Rebels" study, the young people were asking for their right to inhabit a space on their terms.

RACISM IS ENTRENCHED WITHIN THE LANDSCAPE: THE BUS RIDE HOME

Zanib writes: In this section, I provide a reflective piece about how writing has enabled me to name and articulate the racism I have experienced in my life, growing up in Newcastle and then Rotherham, in the United Kingdom, as a Muslim Pakistani-heritage black woman. Through writing, invisible communities can articulate their own marginality. Here I describe my experience as a schoolgirl in 1970s. This experience is entrenched in my consciousness and never forgotten. Racism is ingrained within the landscape (Gillborn and Ladson-Billings 2010). This poem was written in response to an incident in my childhood where the bus driver refused to let me onto a bus on a snowy winter's day in Rotherham, and I had to walk home:

The Bus Ride Home by Zanib

Running out of school like a flock of sheep
Another horrid school day, thankfully over
I get to the bus stop and join my brothers
We stand at the back of the queue, it was safer that way as you did not get your hair pulled or get punched in the back
If you were ethnic minority, you knew your position in the queue, like in life, at the back
The injustice of it all, I have spent half of my life waiting at the end of the queue, but no more
The bus arrives finally, 15 minutes late, slipping and sliding on a very icy road
My class fellows get on the bus, when it's our turn, the door slams quickly before any of us got one foot on the bus
The half-empty bus is driven away by a fat smirking, bulldog-looking bus driver
The indignity of it all, made me think of the civil rights era when black people were made to stand up on buses and give seats to white passengers
The anger heats my blood to a boiling point that I cannot feel the cold anymore
Each step I take in the snow makes my anger grow in to a volcanic explosion
My eyes burn from tears I hold back
We walk through Clifton Park, which looked picturesque, newly fallen white fluffy snow on trees with icicles hanging on branches, a perfect Christmas card and "joy to all men," but I cannot really see the beauty of it today
The world at that moment was very ugly and unkind
An hour and half later we get to our street, tired, miserable, and cold
We walk in to our front room where a warm welcoming, amber red coal fire awaited us
Our little brother and sisters played in a corner, oblivious to the unfairness of life; they would soon find out for themselves how cruel people can be.
Racism never goes away

Rotherham is a town that has seen seventeen Far Right marches in recent years. Racism is like the chameleon: it camouflages itself in many forms, and when the political climate is in turmoil, it shows itself with a vengeance, and another generation of minority children have to endure it. At a time of uncertainty, of political and social upheaval, when people from minority communities are made to feel that they do not belong, writing and poetry are a way for women and young people from these communities to make sense of their world, to articulate their emotions, to build resilience, and to heal themselves.

TRUE STORIES AND COUNTERSTORIES: THE BLOODY BOOTS

Kate writes: In my work, I have explored how over time girls and young women enact their identities in their writing. When I first met her, Lucy was a ten-year-old British Asian girl, living on a small street in central Rotherham with her parents and sisters. She was the eldest of three children. Lucy (the pseudonym she chose does not reflect her heritage) was very shy. As I got to know her, however, I realized that her shy demeanor belied a much fiercer consciousness. From about the age of ten onward, Lucy wrote stories and shared some of these with me. When she entered secondary school, she made sense of the racism in her school through the powerful literary trope of attacking the blonde girl of her story "How to Drown a Blondie" (Pahl 2014b, 304–305). Lucy also wrote a horror story called "Blood Boots" in 2014:

Blood Boots by Lucy

I am going to tell you a story that you may not think is true. But I wouldn't want to waste your time writing a load of garbage, and I am warning you now if you get nightmares if someone tells you a ghost story; immediately put this story down before it is too late for you and you may regret it for the rest of your life! ... Many people had written stories about me, made films and had wrote many articles about me. But they were all twisted round to make it look like I had chopped my own leg off. So I decided to write my own version of this "Breaking News!"

Here Lucy describes her character's fear of not being believed and her decision to set the record straight. Young people's testimonies are often not believed; the rage this experience gives rise to is powerful. The author of "How to Drown a Blondie" wanted to challenge racism in her school. "Blood Boots" was a tale of her reclaiming a story. Lucy's language is direct and confrontational—"you may regret this" and "I decided to write my own version." This "setting the record straight" was very much part of Lucy's focus as a writer.

Two years later, Lucy was still writing. Working with poet Helen Mort and Zanib Rasool on the "Threads of Time" project (described above by Zanib), she wrote about "Lady Walker," the "Lady of the Manor," when visiting Clifton Museum, once the home of the Industrialist Joshua Walker.

Lucy's themes of women's powerlessness and the need to "speak my mind" come up again within this poem:

I am Lady Walker by Lucy

More than a maid but less than an equal to my superior
More than a simple peasant but less than Royal blood
Thy sings and doesn't bathe in mud
Thy is purer than white
Fresh as snow

My purpose is to be pretty
Certainly not witty
I don't speak my mind
Because I'm supposed to be kind
I am oppressed because of my femininity
Oh, I so wish I had more masculinity

They give me flowers
My husband powers
They don't acknowledge me
They only look at me.

Lucy's description of Lady Walker explores how she does not speak her mind and is silenced: "They only look at me." Kelly Wissman and colleagues (2015) write about how the dominant media outlets do not acknowledge much less portray the powerful stories and visions that young girls can create as artists operating in "spaces opening in imagination" (Greene 2000, 293). As Lalitha Vasudevan and Tiffany DeJaynes (2013, 3) write: "The arts have the ability to inspire the as yet uninspired or render visible the unseen." Over the years that Lucy worked with us, her voice was clear and rang out, from her stories at age eleven and her poetry at seventeen:

I Come From by Lucy
I come from Rotherham, my mother too,
My father from the East, very traditionalist and authoritarian
The clash of two cultures, British–Pakistani
Leaves me questioning every action, every thought ...

Opening up a space of possibility is a radical act of hopefulness. Literacies are political (Rogers 2018). Living literacies entwine artwork with words; they provide ways to resituate ways of knowing within communities. Films, poems, and artwork by young people in Rotherham have contributed to the production of public pedagogies (see glossary); exhibitions that have been shown in public libraries and displayed in public spaces (Hickey-Moody 2013). Lucy's writing taught us how to recognize the creative literacies of activism and listen to them.

SCHOOL GATE LITERACIES: RETHINKING ACTIVIST LITERACIES

Zanib writes: Here I describe what I have called "school gate literacies": informal conversations mums have with one another when they drop off their children at school in the morning. They gather in groups outside the school, exchanging community news—the Asian fabric shop is having a sale, for example, or Daz Soap Powder is 20 percent off at the local Morrisons—orally transferring knowledge, sometimes from things they have read. Muslim women, in particular, often share knowledge and keep one another informed in this way. Many women adapt technology to aid their literacy practices in transferring information through oral dialogue to those women who do not read. Indeed, James Paul Gee (2004, 11) argues that oral languages have existed for all human cultures for long enough to become "part of our human biological inheritance." Oral literacy is thus also part of South Asian women's heritage. Wherever women gather, literacy happens through their social exchanges.

Although very few people attach any importance to them, since most consider dropping children off at school to be just another "household chore," the conversations of school gate literacies are often the first steps toward activist literacy (Rasool 2019), which Virginia Crisco (2009, 32) has characterized as "the rhetorical use of literacy for civic participation." Indeed, the school gate can readily become a site for women's activism, which tends to be around local issues, such as seeing that green spaces are available for children to play in, addressing traffic safety problems near schools, and opposing the closing of community libraries or youth centers. Women often become activists to protect their family and community interests. I have heard how the social exchanges of school gate literacy can lead to activism and civic engagement when women remind one another to vote in a local election or attend a community engagement meeting with the police, or when they arrange to go and see their local council member about speeding cars near their school. You do not have to hold a placard and march through the streets of London to be an activist.

But a woman's literacy practices most often happen in the home: writing a shopping list, learning a new recipe from the Internet, listening to her child read a book. Thus Susan Hyatt (2014) found that "the most important and interesting activism occurred in women's homes as part of their everyday lives." But, when women define themselves as housewives and their place as the home, their literacy practices, being private, do not get the same recognition they would if they were in the public domain. and, like school gate literacies, they are largely invisible to others. Speaking of women from my heritage background, however, Parveen Akhtar (2014, 234) has stressed the importance of such private literacy practices in maintaining cultural links to Pakistan: "Women reassembled bits of Pakistani life and culture in the UK through cooking, stories, songs, and the performance of religious rituals." By writing about women's literacy practices in the home or at the school gate, researchers can make both the practices and the activism they lead to visible.

Lyn Tett, Mary Hamilton, and Jim Crowther (2012, 2) remind us that "literacy is deeply and inescapably bound up with producing, reproducing and maintaining unequal arrangements of power." But, for her part, Kathleen Rockhill (1987, 165) has argued that, even though "literacy is caught up in material, racial and sexual oppression of women … it embodies their hope for escape." Indeed, David Barton and Mary Hamilton (2000, 8) contend that "literacy practices are purposeful and embedded in broader social goals and cultural practices."

WEAVING IT ALL TOGETHER: CONCLUDING THOUGHTS

Kate and Zanib write: We have worked together on our coedited book about Rotherham and its hidden histories, *Reimagining Contested Communities* (Campbell et al. 2018)—inspired by Susan Hyatt (2017), who described a collaborative project on the hidden history and material cultures of an urban neighborhood whose past had become invisible. Community activism is a powerful tool for people made invisible by changes in our physical, social, and political landscapes to reclaim their own histories and achieve justice. Our *Re-Imagining Contested Communities* project team (Campbell et al. 2018) drew on Elizabeth Campbell and Eric Lassiter's collaborative approach to ethnography (Campbell and Lassiter 2015; see also Lassiter 2005). Team members were also inspired by *The Other Side of Middletown* (Lassiter et al. 2004), where community activists joined with university faculty to cowrite a book about the African American histories of Middletown (as Muncie, Indiana, is also known). The *Other Side* coauthors were committed to social justice and to cowriting as a practice and drew on traditions of community development and community activism. Coauthoring is complex and difficult, as Joanne Larson and George Moses (2018) attest, but it can create new and emergent forms of knowledge, and it can bring diverse groups together (Banks et al. 2019; Campbell et al. 2018; see also Hanny et al. 2018, 46).

Writing this chapter together has entwined our shared but different voices. It is a trace of our work on the "Imagine" project, where our team invited international researchers such as Elizabeth Campbell and Susan Hyatt to share the research journey, a process that helped us write together (Campbell et al. 2018). But our voices are different. Kate has not experienced racism in the way Zanib has. She has never had a bus driver shut a door in her face, nor has she been told at sixteen that she does not have the right to go on to university. Her whiteness and social class have shaped her life chances. What the two of us do share, however, is our commitment to transformational change in communities. This is a hopeful chapter, but also an angry and uncomfortable one. At a time when political discourses seem to be deteriorating in many countries, *Living Literacies* celebrates multiplicity, dissensus, collective struggle, resistance, and uncomfortable truths, as well as the importance of valuing voice and giving voice to those who have not yet been heard. Cowriting creates a wonderful space to negotiate new ways of knowing and to cocreate shared values of writers advocating for marginalized women. Our two voices come from different vantage points; we each see the world through a different lens. This difference is what has created a unique writing experience, one that weaves together in harmony the different colored threads of the chapter—and that lives and entwines the literacies it presents.

Figure 4.1
"Concrete Utopia" by Steve Pool

4

HOPING: THE LITERACIES OF THE "NOT YET"

Kate Pahl and Steve Pool

But we walk in the forest and we feel we are or could be what the forest dreams.
—Ernst Bloch ([1918] 2000, 34)

In this chapter, we orient living literacies toward hopeful practices—toward thinking through what literacy could be in all its potential. We weave our projects together with visions of literacy practices to conjure up a journey of hope. Believing that living literacies are grounded in practice and located within the everyday of lived experience, we see literacy as emergent, situated in a space of the "not yet." In this chapter, we work with the teachings of German thinker Ernst Bloch, who located many of his ideas within a philosophy of hope and whose books *The Spirit of Utopia* ([1918] 2000) and *The Principle of Hope* ([1954] 1986) open a way of thinking that points us toward hopeful and livable futures (see figure 4.1). We focus on Bloch's idea that daydreaming can open possibilities rich with future potential for change within troubled worlds. We firmly believe that glimmers of hope lie everywhere within the everyday and that this belief is more than wishful thinking.

A hopeful approach to literacy practices helps us see the many threads of the webs of meaning that flow through the past, into the present, and on into all potential futures. A living literacies approach concerns itself with the affective intensities that lie beneath the surface of texts—and that can emerge in the richness and complexities of the everyday (Stewart 2007). Grounded in practice, it requires a broader view of literacy, a view gained by being "with" and traveling alongside those who are doing the crafting, and one that sees and re-visions what is going on (Back 2007). We do not position this "What if ... ?" approach against current approaches as a critique. We see it rather as a proposition: What if we expand the terrain of literacies and work in the hopeful landscapes where it can live forward?

What we are proposing, then, is not a new theory about hopeful literacies, but rather a new approach to recognizing them. Such an approach needs to be open to diversity, to modes of inquiry that are congruent with young people's choices, possibilities, and understandings. Adopting a living literacies approach, young people can share their lived literacies by asking questions, documenting their literacies, and recognizing where literacy sits within their everyday lives. By opening out a future vision of literacies, new possibilities come into play, and the ideological and material shaping of everyday texts is recognized (Hull and Nelson 2009). Literacy spills over into uncharted territories that include political and aesthetic modes of criticality, marking new terrains of resistance to "schooled" literacy practices rooted in the visual and embodied (Enriquez et al. 2016). Our approach centers on the "What if ... ?" and asks how an ever-expanding view of literacy might shape our understandings of meaning-making practices from where we stand.

OUR DEFINITIONS

New Literacy Studies is associated with the work of social anthropologist Brian Street. In a 2006 workshop he facilitated in New Delhi, teachers learned how to help their students recognize script on walls and doorways as literacy practices (Nirantar Collective 2007). Street opened up the concept of "literacy events" to include where literacy was observed coming into being and patterned literacy practices that occurred over time and space. The concept of "literacy events" has been revisited by Cathy Burnett and Guy Merchant (2018, 7) in relation to what is "to come" and what "could be" and is more closely theorized in chapter 6. Here, however, we only note how the events sit with anticipatory practices in the world, which explains how literacy is something coming into being, anticipated but never fully realized or understood—what Bloch describes as the "not yet." Viewed speculatively, literacy is an emergent process and can become something "other," straying into a nonrepresentational space (MacLure 2016). Speculative thinking (see glossary) has enabled literacy work to be located in a sense of what could be (Springgay and Rotas 2014). The literacy event as emergent creates a space of possible practices and enables flows beyond current bounded uses and pedagogies.

New Literacy Studies not only presented a forward-oriented view of emerging literacy practices, but also located these practices within the "becoming" space of possibilities. Unsticking itself from its representational boundaries, the literacy event is remade in each encounter with actors and objects, and, through the "not yet" movement of the event, it enlivens itself. Gunther Kress (1997) tells us that literacy practices are both enacted within sites and spaces and also provisionally and constantly remade. But when meaning-generating interactions are understood to be a form of literacy event, something both written and read, literacy is again reconceived. The living literacy event enables us to ask again what literacy can be.

In this chapter, we build a potential for hopeful literacies by articulating where new spaces of literacy practice can be found, built, and perceived—and felt everywhere. Seeing lived literacy both as orientation and practice, as a way of generating theory through experience, we move from New Literacy Studies into process-oriented models of literacy research.

The idea of hopeful living literacies grew from an encounter—through research with the world. As a researcher and an artist, we have conducted a number of projects together. The moments that stand out in our memories include fragments of poems, groups of children on a summer's day pretending to be Vikings or pirates, building dens—or just being themselves—as well as stories, friendships and daydreams. A hopeful literacy is not located in spelling, sentence structure, or handwriting; it lives in the world of meanings that are alive and mobile, fleeting and free to change and grow.

Our work is centered on our living of literacies in the sites and spaces of our lives. Our discussion focuses on created moments where things felt as if they could be otherwise. Literacy is re-formed in the process of doing and writing, of feeling and yearning toward something new, something half-glimpsed and ephemeral, made in the moment, something not fixed into texts or formed—something not yet said, but already spoken.

To illustrate the emergent nature of literacy, as a researcher and an artist writing together, we describe some moments of our practice with young people, from projects in playgrounds, beside ponds, in schools, and within communities (see "Chapter 4 Featured Studies" in appendix). We link these moments with the thinking of researchers who wish to reimagine pedagogy, from Barbara Comber's site-specific work in Australia to Kris Gutiérrez's future-oriented vision of a pedagogy grounded in a resilient ecology (Comber 2016; Gutiérrez 2016). We argue that work with children and young people that shows them how to recognize their own ways of communicating opens up new ways of seeing literacy practices. Working together, whether in writing a book, making an artwork, or simply playing, offers a shared space of possibility from which relational events and literacies can spring. Our reading of Bloch inspired us to think differently: when we glimpsed literacy events with our eyes "wide-shut," the events became possible moments rather than actual practices. This gave our work an inventive quality, much like that of children when they transform in their text making (Kress 1997).

FUTURES, IMAGINATION, FEELINGS, LITERACIES

In this and the sections that follow, we consider the changing nature of literacy and its "becoming-ness" in the world. We think about stories as a way of describing what we see, orienting to a tradition of telling stories as a way of thinking differently, much like Ernst Bloch ([1930] 2006) or Lauren Berlant and Kathleen Stewart (2019), who use stories to explore the world, to make us think, and to develop theory. Stories can be articulations of the unsaid, of what "could be" as well as of what is. Stories can also be what we tell to explain ourselves. They resonate through what we do over the years, and we think and work with them to live through our ideas (Stewart 2007).

Within young people's stories, emotion plays an important part in their articulation of the future, in aspirations for higher education, for example, as Valerie Harwood and colleagues (2017, 5) have found, stressing the importance of feelings as a way of locating and informing future ideas. Speech and writing are practices of participation and belonging, where certain things can be said beyond what is already there. A living literacies approach acknowledges the importance of literacy as something lived over time. Though associated with particular times, literacy practices move outside as well as within time and are constructed both within and beyond the time of the everyday (Compton-Lilly 2010). Literacy has also been associated with particular scripts and feelings. Within ephemeral small moments of meaning making, literacies that were stitched, traced, drawn, expressed, or typed on a keyboard, small articulations and imaginings of what "could be" appeared. These were shaped and informed both aesthetically politically; through this process, narratives of resistance appeared. Expressions of hope are culturally located, within existing fragments, texts, stories, and cultural narratives (Boggs, Duarte, and Manglitz 2017).

FISHING AND YOUTH WORK

> And an ingenious Spaniard says, that "rivers and the inhabitants of the watery element are made for wise men to contemplate, and for fools to pass by without consideration."
>
> —Izaak Walton and Charles Cotton ([1653] 2008, 40–41)

Walton and Cotton's *The Compleat Angler*, a text written in seventeenth-century England to describe the pleasures of fishing, inspired a project that looked to fishing as a form of wisdom. Reading the original text, the team realized that fishing was not a metaphor, but a complete way of being in the world. Our project involved taking a group of young people fishing together with older anglers (coaches) and youth workers (see "Communicating Wisdom" under "Chapter 4 Featured Studies" in appendix). Guided by their older coaches, the young people learned to fish, and the entire research team engaged with the wisdom and beauty involved in fishing. Having explored why fishing made life better by making a series of short films about fishing, the young people concluded that it did so by creating a space to be still and quiet. Kirsty, aged 13, had this to say:

> The thing with fishing, projects like this, it gets kids off the street instead of—kids my age can be sat by the side of the [pond] instead of being out late at night. When they are sat by the side of the riverbank they are like, admiring the nature of the place. Fishing ain't gonna solve a problem but for the amount of time you are doing fishing it takes your mind off a problem, because it's focusing on what you are doing. (Kirsty, November 2013)

The older angler coaches told stories about fishing to the young people, whose skills they valued. Team member Hugh Escott captured this interaction between them:

> Terry spoke at length about coaching and fishing. Especially about how you can tell in 5 minutes if someone has a natural talent for snooker or football but you can't tell if someone will be a natural fisher. He spoke of people he knows who aren't "very bright" but were incredible fishermen. All the while he was watching over Reece's shoulder and discussing what he was doing with him. Reece joined in with what he thought about certain aspects of fishing. Reece spoke to me for a while about his success in match fishing and his preference for carp fishing, which Terry also preferred. (Hugh Escott, field notes, April 23, 2013)

Although the skills of fishing are hidden, when they were framed as literacy, ways of communicating could be considered differently. Fishing became a process of making sense and learning through the experience of sitting by the pond and spending time together. Our knowing was informed by the site and practice of fishing. From this came oral stories and appreciation of the process. Kirsty expressed this beautifully:

> Fishing helps you because it calms you down when you are sat there. What I found, with the pond, when I was watching it, I was really calm just watching the water. When it were like spitting a little bit it looked amazing on the water because it was so peaceful, you could see the little rings just spreading out. (Kirsty, discussion, November 2013)

Fishing became a way of exchanging knowledge and a way of creating calming spaces as well as a site of storying, an aesthetically informed and embodied experience of beauty and a passing on of oral heritage and lore (Pahl et al. 2017). The literacies of fishing were about cocreating knowledge across generations, with the older anglers passing on their skills to the young people, who, in turn, had new ways of knowing that the older anglers learned from. Some of the young people were themselves expert fishers. Here is how Kate described one such fisher:

> I decided to sit on the bank and watch Dylan (aged 13). Dylan sat very still. He dropped his line very low in the water. He watched and did not do anything else, speak or chat or move. Every so often, he would catch a fish and he would bring it in, carefully, inspect it, take the hook out, and throw it back in. Once or twice, he needed the landing net. When he caught a fish, he drew it in quietly and gently. He did not boast or show other people. It was part of the process of fishing. (Kate Pahl, field notes. June 4, 2013)

This echoes Barbara Comber's suggestion (2016, 150) to think about what young people could –and can—do: "What if these temporal and spatial frames were altered to take on literacy as a socio-spatial accomplishment of people working together?"

An appreciation of collective literacies opens up a pedagogical space that recognizes what young people can do. The interaction between the older anglers, the young people, and the written, oral, and multimodal texts that were produced in "Communicating Wisdom: Fishing and Youth Work" all came from a relational sense of purpose—to engage in fishing. Literacy became embedded in "the new collaborations, stories, conceptualizations, directions, intentions and so on that emerge as people engage in making meanings" (Burnett and Merchant 2018, 8).

That these meaning-making practices are diverse, multimodal, and material feeds the idea of "dynamic literacies" that are assembled to create new forms of belonging (Potter and McDougall 2017)—literacies that involve gesture, emotion, bodies, and space (Leander and Boldt 2013, Enriquez et al. 2016). These paradigms open out and reach across one another to make literacy an expansive concept.

The fishing project situated language and literacy by a pond and allowed for expression to flow from that experience. The young people's own language shifted as they described the beauty and stillness of the pond. Kirsty's poetic language opens up the opportunity to think about how pedagogies could be located differently, how they could create a stronger repertoire for the literacies of place. An expansive understanding of colearning and cocreation can offer pedagogical pathways that are grounded in sites and spaces that are both about the here and now and oriented toward the future.

WHAT COULD LITERACY BE?

A hopeful literacies orientation can expand the boundaries of what literacy could be—a literacy whose forms might change in response to what is needed to make meaning (Finnegan 2015). Literacies are on the move, and their practices are shifting. The question then becomes "What are the new aesthetic contours of literate practices beyond reading, writing, speaking, and listening?" (Vasudevan and DeJaynes 2013, 5). Literacy, when expanded across the stuff of life, can become entangled within other modes—gestural, oral, visual—and can emerge changed and transformed in the process. Literacy becomes linked to affective structures that can elude representational practice (Ehret 2018b).

In this chapter, we see the arts as a place-based materialization from which a response to the present can be pursued and a lens created through which to explore young people's textual productions. Kelly Wissman and colleagues (2015) argue that literacy research processes could be shifted and opened out through a better understanding of the literacies produced by young people. This would create a space to reimagine the futures of literacy as being concerned with what John Potter and Julian McDougall (2017, 15) describe as "dynamic literacies" that are complex and future oriented, incorporating a myriad of digital and multimodal ways of communicating—literacies that are "both *synchronic,* inclusive of current situated practices, and *diachronic,* a term which opens the possibility of movement through time as an incorporated principle" (Potter and McDougall, 2017, 36).

Literacy in this understanding appears nested within other things on the move, which include artistic forms such as visual art, poetry, and built sculptures. In our research studies, small pieces of text made up the contours of a multilingual, collectively produced art image of a Union Jack (see figure 4.4). Poetry became a mode of expression and an opportunity to write scripts of hope as well as resistance.

This approach to literacy lets everybody —adults, children, and young people alike—encounter the materially created textual objects, woven and sewn, digital, material and (im)material, that they observe (Burnett, Merchant, et al. 2014). The process of recognizing a literacy event is thus made accessible to people outside academia and includes the collective framing of literacy and what it could become. Candace Kuby, Tara Gutshall Rucker, and Jessica Kirchhofer (2015) call this kind of thinking "literacy desiring," which, having collectively situated, produced, and reproduced literacy, reaches out across modalities and across objects to reanimate a relational account of how literacy could be.

DOES MONEY MAKE YOU HAPPY OR SAD?

Joe Orton was a rebellious British writer famously prosecuted for defacing library books. But when he defaced their covers by collaging them with new, often scatological meanings, he did so artistically, thus his name is associated with art as well as protest. In this story of defaced library books, the form became a springboard for a re-visioning project. Many of Kate's projects were conducted in community libraries, with the support of friendly community librarians, hot chocolate, and lots of young people, who came to the library to roller-skate, talk, hang out, and read (Pahl and Allan 2011). As part of a study exploring home writing practices (see "Writing in the Home and in the Street" under "Chapter 4 Featured Studies" in appendix), Kate was working with a small group of young people who attended a community library to explore their views of what a "better childhood" could look like through a focus on everyday literacies. She was sitting in a room in the library, equipped with craft materials including a paint pot and a lift the flap book, talking to two twelve-year-old girls. She watched with some concern as the girls took hold of the toddler book and slowly began to paint over it. With paint, pens, and glue, they set about repurposing the toddler book into a manual for teenagers, keeping its lift the flap format, but matching its content to that of teenage magazines. On one of the pages of the repurposed book, they asked, "Does money make you happy or sad? Now's the time to decide" (see figure 4.2), thus presenting a double-voiced future in which possibilities were immanent within a text. When Kate went to report what the girls had done, the librarian cheerfully said they had another copy, and it was fine that the girls had turned the lift the flap book for toddlers into one for teenagers. In this work with young people, literacy slipped back and forth in time. Fixed within the "lift the flaps" of the toddler book, it was also articulated in the repurposed book as a future-oriented question about what money meant to teenage readers; it shifted and was revisited in the process.

In thinking about the literacies of the repurposed toddler book, now used by teenagers, meaning making becomes about the potentials for lived life—about the potentials of the literacy event that not only foreground how certain relations sustain but also how those relations might be otherwise imagined. It is a stance that leans toward new possibilities, "etching out new kinds of relations even within apparently highly structured sites" (Burnett and Merchant 2018, 8). Thus the story here is not only about what could be, but also about the process of creating and making, where thinking and meaning are entwined within the processes of imagining and becoming:

Figure 4.2
"Does Money Make You Happy or Sad?" Photo credit: Kate Pahl

To tap into imagination is to become able to break with what is supposedly fixed and finished, objectively and independently real. It is to see beyond what the imaginer has called normal or "common-sensible" and to carve out new orders in experience. Doing so, a person may become freed to glimpse what might be, to form notions of what should be, and what is not yet. And the same person may, at the same time, remain in touch with what presumably *is*. (Greene 2000, 19).

Maxine Greene's remarks about imaginative thought provide a language of description for locating the literacies of hope. If we speculate that literacies are situated in the sites and spaces from which they are generated, then literacy can live within everyday events. When seen through a lens of a hopeful living literacy, this can mean more than finding meaning within our lives; it can also mean writing into and reading the world.

SHARING STORIES, BECOMING PIRATES

As part of a study researching artists' contributions to social cohesion, Steve built a pirate ship (see figure 4.3) to create a new play space within an adventure playground (see "Taking Yourself Seriously" under "Chapter 6 Featured Studies" in appendix). As the research developed, the pirate ship played a number of symbolic roles. For the playground staff, it represented an external acknowledgment of and investment in young people's rights to play. For the study researchers, it represented a commitment to putting something back into the community they were working with that aligned with the core aims of the playground. For Steve, as an artist, it was a symbolic way to put himself into the mix of research, to build and make, spend time with people, and share stories of working lives. And for the children, it represented something different happening, a new set of possibilities, new routes around the playground, somewhere to play, to act out, and to hide. This real and symbolic pirate ship could be imagined

Figure 4.3
Pirate ship. Photo credit: Steve Pool

as a focal point for literacies, including the oral stories and play of the children and the new calluses on Steve's hands. It also appears in more traditional texts in the words and writing of the play workers through text messages and research paper presentations. The writing included grant proposals, newspaper columns, and Steve's own work about being part of the playground project in blogs and oral stories.

The symbolic threads cannot stop there; as with any text, meaning spills out into an expanded view of space that takes into account different trajectories. The visionary educationalist Colin Ward (1973) saw the "adventure playground" as a potential space of hope, of anarchy in action. Essentially evolving from the physical and mental devastation of the Second World War, the Adventure Play Movement finds its origin within a utopian vision, a hope that personal renewal and a more just social order could emerge through unregulated play. The building of dens and towers on former bomb sites generated small and temporary communities of purpose—spaces for "pro-sociality," where the scars of the landscape met the ruins of lost childhoods, places of forward dreaming, creative actions, and making. A team member from the Pitsmoor Adventure Playground described the benefits of unregulated play:

> It creates a sense of harmony and cooperation and cohesion. It is a unique space where everybody comes collectively together regardless of their beliefs, of their age, and their abilities and they all contribute. Lots of it is about arts, crafts, play and having fun. But more importantly, celebrating each other's culture, and giving people a sense of place and they all have a sense of place here, ownership. It's their playground, it isn't ours, we just facilitate some of the play. (Patrick Meleady, play worker at the adventure playground, Sheffield, June 2016)

Each play worker, child, parent, artist, or volunteer, brought his or her own fund of knowledge to the playground. Thinking about what a pirate ship might mean, the research team had to consider what it could represent. At various points, the team worried about the experience at sea of Syrian refugees, confrontations with pirates off the coast of Somalia, and the "Windrush scandal" over the UK Home Office's denial of citizenship to British subjects who came mostly on ships to build their lives in the United Kingdom. All the threads that connected ships or boats to people became part of a greater text of consideration. During the last week of construction work on the pirate ship, Steve got a phone call from his dad, who had just had the results of a liver biopsy. At that point, the prognosis did not look good, and this, too, became inscribed into the making of the ship.[1]

Expanding a literacy event to include all its potential relations sets all symbolic actions, all exchanges of meaning, into an ever-expanding context. Meaning can be gleaned from the constant flows and interactions—but never really fixed.

MOVING LITERACY ON THROUGH PLAY

In the context of the playground, movement, action, building, making, and play as imaginative storytelling become the seeds for literacy. By paying attention to the literacy event and the sites and spaces that create it, hopeful literacies are born. Play, building, and making are imaginative tools that encourage forward thinking. These living literacies rest on action, on the sites and spaces from which they come, and are generated in moments of making that are grounded in the everyday. From these moments, interactions—oral, written and gestural—come into play as literacy.

It could be argued, following Colin Ward (1973), that emergent literacies can form and develop along the lines of a functioning anarchic community. If a community could use and develop its own literacy tools, literacy itself could change. This would let us see how unregulated or less structured approaches to literacy could evolve far deeper levels of understanding and communication—how we could evolve literacy practices that collectively move toward understanding, in contrast to state-controlled, systemically taught literacies and language. This hopeful approach to literacy requires an element of daydreaming, a distancing from the preconceptions and modes of thinking that keep us from seeing how we might build something better.

Reconceptualizing literacy in a site-specific way means paying attention to the specific materialities and modes of where things happen, whether in a backyard, in a forest, or on a pirate ship. From these spaces,

---

1. At this writing, Steve's dad is still with us and healthy; the pirate ship is named *The Lucky Gordon* in honor of his continued vitality.

literacies are born and new scripts developed. Our collective work on the playground took the form of dispersed literacy practices across several research studies (see "Chapter 4 Featured Studies" in appendix). We wrote about our adventure playground in articles in the local newspaper and in reports submitted to a select committee of the House of Lords on civic engagement. Our playground generated literacies through its own songs and sayings, scripts of play, and unintended interactions between children and across generations.

Literacy is entwined with the everyday but stands apart as textual, incorporating both writing and speech. Its textuality is its purpose, and as it moves across sites and spaces, it fixes and unfixes, becomes material and (im)material in the making of meaning (Burnett, Merchant, et al. 2014). In contrast to school-based literacy practices, the expanded view of meaning making that emerged through these projects gave rise to a temporal yet nonsequential encounters with writing and reading folded into space that were constantly in movement.

UTOPIAN VISIONS OF LITERACY RESEARCH

Recognizing, with Brian Street, the challenge of thinking differently, New Literacy Studies offered an expansive view of literacy, through noticing what was going on. By expanding the idea of what literacy is, it became possible to begin breaking down the ideological approaches that dictated its teaching and uses. And by focusing on the uses of literacy (after Hoggart 1957), a more open understanding emerged: literacy as lived within an event—as present but also unfolding, also to come. The ideological model requires that we recognize "the variety of cultural practices associated with reading and writing in different contexts,", avoid reification, but focus instead on "social practices rather than literacy-in-itself" (Street 1993a, 7). In this way, literacy is positioned as an emergent, rather than a static, concept, opening the way for people outside academia to become researchers. Doing research as a practice of knowing, so that theory derives from practice, has a utopian quality since it is predicated upon change.

A utopian view of literacy has implications for curriculum and pedagogy. Although what "could be" lies in understanding what children and young people are currently doing, it can be enacted in pedagogies of possibility, built from children's lived experience, but enacted within complex social, material, and communicational environments (Comber 2016). These pedagogies operate both in the present and in the future, which is "distinguished by its grammar of hope, possibility, and resilience" (Gutiérrez 2016, 188); they "require *being in the moment* with youth, and imagining together what youth can do and who they are becoming" (Ehret 2018a, 56; italics in original).

Working with young people to collectively imagine what could be emphasizes speculation and affect, emergent modes of thinking that challenge autonomous accounts of literacy (Truman 2019). Experiencing new ideas involves change, for literacy researchers and practitioners alike: "We all have to live with the psychological and social consequences of the new theories" (Street 1997, 52).

Being open to "new theories" and attentive to what "could be" has implications for literacy in theory as well as in practice. Critical literacy education researcher Ernest Morrell (2017) stresses the urgency of reimagining literacy if we are to cocreate the literacies of the future; he advocates for a literacies education grounded in its commitment to equality. Thinking with young people is about "becoming different" (Ehret 2018a, 56), where thinking *with* is also thinking *ahead*. It involves considering a "politics-to-come," which entails "thinking about pedagogy from the perspective of movement, as an elastic force and as knowing that cannot be foreseen or predicted in advance" (Rotas and Springgay 2013, 278). A perspective of "unknowing" (Vasudevan 2011) can enable change to happen differently, creating shared and collaborative cothinking with young people in open, productive, emergent places and offering a literacy of resistance. Cathy Burnett and Guy Merchant (2018, 7) argue that "the act of writing then involves the ongoing realization of potentialities, many of which may never have been consciously apparent beforehand." This "ongoing realization of potentialities" brings with it a force of newness, of the unexpected, which is key to a hopeful vision of literacies.

Young people already participate in literacies of belonging and the imagination, which, though they do not always translate across into mainstream schooling, could be articulated in future orientations and identities. Planning and articulating futures depend both on pedagogies of possibility (Comber 2016) and on recognizing possible literacies as ways for young people to become active agents in the world. New Literacy Studies recognizes that the realm of literacy practices is vast, reaching far outside the realm of what is currently considered to be literacy and that we have looked at only a tiny part of that realm. A hopeful literacies approach reaches out to enable more of it to become visible.

STORYING THE UNION JACK

Kate's projects often happen by accident or happenstance. Meeting with artist Shaheen Shah and researcher Zanib Rasool, together with community worker Mariam Shah, in Shaheen's house in Rotherham one March afternoon led to a moment of collective daydreaming (see "Threads of Time" under "Chapter 3 Featured Studies" for details). This was three months before the EU referendum. Our brief was to cocreate a project about utopia and hope. We decided that to represent the literacies of hope through collective artwork. A group of Roma Pakistani–heritage girls met in a community center in central Rotherham. With the help of

Figure 4.4
Union Jack artwork by Shaheen Shah

artist Shaheen Shah, the group created a collaborative artwork, a multilingual image of the Union Jack. Within the artwork, located identities in images of familiar local and national symbols, such as the football stadium, a post box, and the crown symbolizing the British monarchy, jostled with more personal inscriptions of identities, such as images of flowers, hearts, hennaed hands, and jewelry.

The artwork became a symbolic space; displayed in exhibitions in Rotherham and at the University of Sheffield, it offered a hopeful vision of a national identity, one that encompassed many different visions of how things could be and how things were. The artwork that the young people and Shaheen created opened up a new space of difference that was honest and concrete but also future oriented and hopeful: it was full of variations, of color, vision, conception, and form; it engaged with tropes as varied as the telephone box and hennaed hands. And, even though it did not of course "solve" the problems of racism, the Union Jack artwork was created in a moment of shared, collective making. The girls who made it came together to celebrate it on an afternoon of tea and cakes, and when it returned home, they donated it to their local high school for permanent display.

As a kind of symbolic, forward-thinking creativity, hopeful imagining offers resistance to prescriptive scripts that close down the reimagining of identity and community (Willis 2000). In taking hold of forms such as collective art making, young people were able to articulate new scripts linked to symbolic creativity and the common, everyday cultures of hope (Williams 1961; Willis 2000). The idea of "culture as ordinary" from Raymond Williams ([1958] 1989) brings the concept of "hopeful imagining" alive. Charles Taylor (2004) writes of the "social imaginaries" that constitute global discourses and circulate in powerful ways. The idea of making stories differently is possible through a radical otherness of possibility. Maxine Greene speaks of the crucial role of imagination:

> One of the reasons I have come to concentrate on imagination as a means through which we can assemble a coherent world is that imagination is what, above all, makes empathy possible. It is what enables us to cross the empty spaces between ourselves and those we teachers have called "other" over the years (Greene 2000, 3).

One of our key challenges today is not only to live with people who think differently from how we think, but also to develop a creative imagination about the other possible worlds that different thinking reflects. The idea of the social imagination can reframe how we think about the world by creating "a mode of utopian thinking: thinking that refuses mere compliance, that looks down roads not yet taken to the shapes of a more fulfilling social order, to more vibrant ways of being in the world" (Greene 2000, 5).

This kind of reshaping of the imagination may be released through thinking about the world in terms of dialogue. By creating possibilities for openness and divergence (see glossary) in hitherto closed or cramped spaces, coproduction offers a utopian space where reimagining could be possible (Bell and Pahl 2018). Many of our projects have been cocreated by community partners who themselves have formed ideas that have transformative potential.

ART AND HOPEFUL LITERACIES

What are the arenas where hopeful literacies can become realized? Art is almost certainly one such arena—one where the dominant and repressive ideas of literacy pedagogies can be legitimately challenged. Artists draw attention to the spaces that get forgotten; they shine a light on the incidental things and bring these into focus. Cultural making practices and cultural forms such as poetry, music, and visual art offer opportunities to reimagine the everyday, and they contribute to new ways of thinking and knowing when life feels unhopeful. Jacques Rancière (2010; Corcoran, 14–15) highlighted the importance of aesthetic freedom and the role of the arts in unleashing the power of transformative and creative action. The practice of art can invite possibility thinking and present an opportunity to think differently (Craft 2013).

Public pedagogies are practices that enable learning within the built environment: in public and community spaces, in museums and art galleries (Ellsworth 2005; Hickey-Moody 2013). Elizabeth Ellsworth (2005, 3–4) talks about the need to find ways of describing experience, about "concepts and languages that will grasp, without freezing or collapsing, the fluid, continuous, dynamic, multiple, uncertain, nondecomposable qualities of experience in the making." She argues that affect and sensation are material and part of this engagement; that the experience of learning involves leaning toward "previously unknown ways of thinking and being in the world"; and that the "space in between" and the "becoming space" are key to an understanding of bodies in motion and the potential vision of pedagogy and places of learning (Ellsworth 2005, 4, 16, 23). Making this process concrete was one of the tasks we were concerned with when we thought about hopeful literacies and the practice of art.

We grounded this vision in our own practice in a project that looked at children's reasons to write (see "A Reason to Write" under "Chapter 6 Featured Studies" in appendix for details). We asked the children to research the ways in which artists worked in schools. They came up with the idea that the artists' work involved "messing about," and, indeed, Marc Lamont Hill and Lalitha Vasudevan (2008) have found that "messing about" can lead to creative play. For the young people in this study, however, messing about was really in-between time, when they could become and be themselves—when they were really present. This study shined a light on a different type of learning and communication, one that felt ancient and natural, undervalued and misunderstood.

Our interest in the role of the artist in school is connected to artist-in-residence programs, where resident artists may be willing to develop shared work—or to provoke new ideas and different thinking. One of the aspects of the artists' subjectivity that we have written about (Pahl and Pool 2018) is the idea of artist as "incidental person," which draws on ideas from the British Artist Placement Group (APG) in the 1960s, which placed resident artists in industry and government workplaces, where they could blend into and become part of their surroundings and not need to produce anything.

Artists can create spaces that are less defined, that concentrate on the small scale and the overlooked in meaning making. As part of a project exploring the use of the arts in education (see "Community Arts Zone" under "Chapter 4 Featured Studies" in appendix), we worked with a group of young children using artistic methodologies to explore their embodied and tacit ways of knowing (Hackett et al. 2017). Drawing on the work of scholars such as Hillevi Lenz Taguchi (2011) and Pauliina Rautio (2013) who value the small and ephemeral work that young children do when they make meaning, we described a kind of blurring in what was going on. Indeed, literacy as a blurred concept can offer a way of knowing that is particularly useful for work with young children. But in the space of the research, children's meaning making was also a space of emergence and *not* knowing. Lalitha Vasudevan (2011, 1158) identifies the important role of "unknowing" in opening a space where new things can emerge in the process of learning:

> Each time we perceive, and as our conceptions become alternatively sedimented and fluid, what—norms, cultural practices, social inclusions and exclusions, assumptions about meaning, stories (of migration, education, justice, incarceration ...)—are we cultivating and nurturing into and out of existence? What is to become of what we do not see? That we are unable to see? Unwilling or unprepared to see? That we do not want to see? As we strive to see, what do we allow ourselves to recognize? As we find comfort in the familiar, how might we see in the unfamiliar a glimmer of recognition?

If we are to recognize and work with differences, it is important *not* to know. By placing the "not yet' in the center of practice, art can open opportunities for making but also remaking across generations (Hickey-Moody 2013, 146–147). Part of this process is to look at what is *not* possible and what is *not* seen: "The arts have the ability to inspire the as yet uninspired or render visible the unseen" (Vasudevan and DeJaynes 2013, 3).

In our work with young people, we have considered how daydreaming, understood by Bloch as an anticipatory practice, can lift us away from the present into an imagined future. Art "shows us the way without alien means, shows us our historically inner path as a flame in which not only the vibrating air but we ourselves begin to tremble and throw off our coats" (Bloch, [1918] 2000). Bloch's work ([1954] 1986) marks the way for our thinking about building concrete utopia, a "not yet" in the making. A sense of imagination is what guides us in this process and takes us back to the moment of creative practice.

PEDAGOGIES OF HOPEFUL LITERACIES

What would hopeful literacies look like in pedagogical practice? Barbara Comber (2016) urges educators to think beyond definitions of literacy to explore what literacy really is and to imagine what it could be. And Brian Street (1993a) invites us to collectively redefine literacy practices with a focus on making life better. For her part, Sarah Truman (2019, 124) writes of the necessity of supporting "revolutionary actions [that] can take the form of minor literacies that disrupt existing ways of thinking about literacy and educative practices." Included among these "minor literacies" could be moments where things are imagined otherwise, where a different world is glimpsed from the corner of an eye. Anna Hickey-Moody (2013, 147) has described the importance of "little publics" that can give rise to aesthetically focused communities across generations. And, in her work on learning ecologies, Kris Gutiérrez (2016, 190) has asked us to consider and design interventions that are both historically grounded and future oriented, to picture and model modes of imaginative thinking that go beyond representation, that open out an expansive model of literacies. Cultural materialism enables pedagogies that are imaginative, moving, emergent, breathing, and intimate. Stephanie Springgay and Nikki Rotas (2014, 13) view the classroom as a work of art, which opens up the idea of a "politics-to-come," where encounters and affective experience become the stuff of pedagogies in the here and now. The question "What … if?" can then orient us to future thinking and create a space of possibility thinking as well.

CONCLUSION

In this chapter, we have offered different ways of enacting pedagogies of hopeful literacies that are specific to the time and place in which they were made—innovative and inspiring pedagogies that respond to their particular communities. We have traced a thread of anticipated hopeful literacies across our research study projects. And, starting with the invitation from New Literacy Studies to "think through" literacy, we asked: What if we could see literacy as a more expansive, more hopeful concept, one linked not only to schooling but also to the everyday? A pirate ship, a fishing trip, a Union Jack, storytelling, playing, and re-visioning within art and poetry can open up new stories where literacy is embedded in the everyday world of actions and space. We then turned to the potential of art as a space of hopefulness in which to locate this reimagined literacy, and to apply it to young people's meaning making.

Our work is speculative, unfinished, and the stuff of memory and dreams. But, even more important, the *concept* of literacy is itself also unfinished. This has implications for pedagogies that can then be built on an expansive view of literacy and codiscovered as part of learning. Such pedagogies require a coproduced approach to research, one whose joint conceptualizations of literacy with children and young people equalize power. Work grounded in utopian and imaginative practice gives us glimpses of new practices that can challenge present rhetorics of despair. We argue for a literacy grounded in the "not yet," one that grows and that expands literacies not only for schoolchildren but also for all people who will shape and use those literacies. We all need the opportunities to imagine other worlds—and literacy itself can be reimagined when we do.

Figure 5.1
Ways of knowing in PicCollage app

5

KNOWING: THE LITERACIES OF DIGITAL AND NONDIGITAL SPACES

Diane Collier and Jennifer Rowsell

The recurrent social practices of everyday life, with their technological tools and embodied human relationships, with their organized actions, their enacted values, and their interpretive norms—these are what make learning possible, from a sociocultural point of view.
—Anne Haas Dyson (2008, 121)

In this chapter, we examine the digital and nondigital texts young people use both to think and to forge new and innovative ways of knowing the world (see figure 5.1). People today often know and engage in knowledge work through digital texts. To live literacies thus entails moving across digital as well as nondigital spaces, and engaging in knowledge work naturally entails, as Dyson (2008) has noted, moving across technical and nontechnical texts, environments, and tools to enact the recurrent practices of everyday life.

Our chapter spotlights "Visualizing Families," an ethnographic research study we conducted together in 2016 at an elementary school in the Niagara region of Ontario, Canada (see "Chapter 5 Featured Study" in appendix). Focusing on family photographs, specifically, on the ways families visualize themselves, what these ways signal about how they think, and the often-invisible literacies they engage in as part of their everyday lives, we explored how schoolchildren moved across digital and nondigital worlds. The visual in figure 5.1, a collage designed by a schoolgirl that displays favorite photos of her family as she sees them, illustrates the kinds of digital literacy practices the research study children engaged in.

"Knowing," as we define it here, represents the ways that people think through digital and nondigital environments and the ways they build literacy practices through their engagement with technologies as they constantly move in and out of print and digital texts. In order to adopt a living literacies approach, it is necessary to fold in digital-, media-, and print-based worlds as shaping the practices of everyday life. These worlds signify particular ways of thinking and being.

People "write" texts in digital environments in vastly different ways, always involving two or more modes in play (Abrams 2014; Kress 2010). Words, images, symbols, and sounds evoke or convey the meanings we want, need, or seek to share, sometimes in themselves as displayed or reproduced, sometimes as connected by hypertext links to other words, images, symbols, and sounds. Often modes combine as converged media (Jenkins 2006) that provide necessary information, such as Google Maps: if we are lost, the visuals and vocal prompts help us locate where we are and where we want to go. Knowledge is augmented and altered in digital worlds in powerful, tacit ways (Hayles 2008). Christian Ehret (2018a) describes these new ways of knowing as "becoming-with technologies." Living literacies through digital means is frequently a personal and idiosyncratic process depending on what we like, gravitate to, and have access to (Morrell and Rowsell 2019).

RESEARCH CONTEXT

We worked together with a grade 4 teacher from January to June 2016 on a family photo research study (see appendix). Diane is a scholar who explores the everyday cultural resources that children engage in at home, with a particular focus on white working-class children and the ways they perform their identities within material worlds (Collier 2015). Gradually, over six months of fieldwork, she came to take part in classroom conversations and the reading of picture books about families, during which time she shared her own family photos and eventually invited Jennifer in over six weeks to share her family photos as well. On several research projects together, the two of us have worked closely with young people as they made texts and engaged in relational practices (see Perry, Collier, and Rowsell 2019).

The larger project within which "Visualizing Families" was situated looked at configurations of changing Canadian families and changing family photography practices. During our research study, schoolchildren and their families chose family photos to share and to work with in class. The photos that families and children chose to represent themselves were focused around happy times, scenes of togetherness, special occasions, birthdays, weddings, and family trips; in other words, photos that present quite normative pictures of what families *should* look like (i.e., happy, celebratory, smiling). In their studies of family photo taking, sociologists like Annette Kuhn (2010) and Gillian Rose (2010, 2012) have noted that the ways that photos are displayed and shared—which photos parents and children select together and how families are presented in them—may be as important as the memories the photos evoke, the potential for sharing family stories they offer, and the analyses of the photos themselves. Here we focus on a group of schoolchildren, the ways particular practices and images circulated among them, and how the children presented their notions of family by playing, thinking, and becoming with family photos through their movement across digitized and material tools. A number of scholars who have researched children's everyday meaning making and playing with everyday texts—like Anne Haas Dyson (2003), Deborah Hicks (2002), Marjorie Siegel (2006), and Pippa Stein (2008)— have found children's individual literacy practices to be agentive and unique. Similarly, in our research, we explored how children in a grade 4 class both idealized and subverted middle-class, normed versions of "the happy family" to make their digital and nondigital texts more authentic and lived.

VISUALIZING LIFE AND FAMILIES

Although photographs are often seen as authentic representations of everyday life, upon closer inspection, it becomes clear that they can invite as many questions about what is *not* photographed as they can about what is. Visuals offer insights that words do not, and they help shift away from linguistic explanations (Mitchell 2011; Pink and Leder Mackley 2014). Indeed, visuals can offer more freedom for learners who either do not like or feel unmotivated by linguistic texts. This chapter examines the visual centrally and the digital tangentially because the digital is a part of a larger web of meaning making we observed over the course of our research. Though not pivotal to it, the digital is embedded in the fabric of a living literacies approach; it feeds into new and innovative ways of knowing and being for young people.

Family photos answer questions such as "What is a happy family?" Normative, sanctioned, and performative versions of family often predominate in family photos, even though the nature of families has changed and continues to change. Images of families, particularly those widely shared and valued, continue to be overwhelmingly normative, representing happiness, togetherness, and special events or milestones based on white middle-class values. Coming from both white and ethnically diverse low-income families, the group of schoolchildren featured in the chapter often used memes and tropes in clever ways to retell and remake family stories within their multimodal compositions. Their productive and agentive ways of knowing took the form of disrupting and poking fun at normalized discourses through memes and remixed digital and nondigital texts. We highlight these practices as key to a living literacies approach and as fundamental to contemporary ways of knowing in digital and nondigital environments.

When Diane told them that family photographs would be part of their unit of study, children in the class brought in photographs that depicted classic and performative pictures of family life. We characterized photographs of this kind as "Hallmark card" presentations of families during holiday events and birthdays. We sought everyday pictures of the children's home lives, as they saw them. We wanted the children to question and to "unknow" (Vasudevan 2011), even to abandon, such normative notions of family on holidays or during special events and, instead, to embrace a more lived picture of their family life. To help them transition into what Lalitha Vasudevan (2011) calls an "unknowing state," we brought in our own quirky photos of family moments such as Diane's photo of herself sitting on a dock away from her other family members in an obviously grumpy mood and Jennifer's photo of herself as a toddler in diapers grabbing a fishing rod while her sister looks on surprised and shocked nearby. The children laughed at these photographs and began to bring in quirky photos of their own, such as one schoolgirl's photo of herself with her dad in a tank top holding a raccoon. Our research team celebrated such moments, which inspired a wide range of funny and clever forms of remixing and memes.

We premised our theorizing of knowing on Lalitha Vasudevan's work on "unknowing" (2011), coupled with Catherine Beavis's and Jennifer's work on new digital epistemologies (Beavis 2014a, 2014b; Rowsell 2014). It took time for the grade 4 schoolchildren to move away from the "Hallmark card" happy family trope and accept alternative framings, and it took time for them to appreciate a more *lived* approach to learning, thinking, and knowing (Whitty 2015), as well as for them to get to know and trust the two of us. Our research offered ways to explore how schoolchildren know and enact literacy practices on technologies like computer tablets and through videogame play in original "becoming-with technologies" ways (Ehret 2018a). We offer our readers ways of "unknowing" as "an invitation to wrest our modes of inquiry and our beings away from the clutches of finite definitions of knowledge and instead rest our endeavors in the beauty of myriad ways of knowing" (Vasudevan 2011, 1157). Contemporary ways of knowing across digital and nondigital domains must therefore include not only formal learning environments like schooling but also, and perhaps most important, informal environments like the home, the street, and the community. So it is that all of us need to "unknow" more traditional framings of our ways of knowing.

RESEARCH BACKGROUND

Our research took place in a classroom of a low-income community school in the Niagara region of Ontario. Over six months, as our study's main adult researchers, we and a grade 4 teacher talked with the schoolchildren in her classroom about their families. We read the children's literature that featured these families—which were often racialized and of diverse composition (e.g., single parent, same-sex parents, multiple generations), and we discussed their family photos and our own. We chose this particular classroom of schoolchildren because Diane had been working with teachers at that community school for several years, the schoolroom teacher was open to our study's inquiry process, and the school was invested in continuing to build relationships with families in a socioeconomic setting where parents often felt unable to contribute to their children's schooling. In our talks with the children, we discussed our research, what research looks like, and how they might become co-researchers in our work together. We cultivated this co-research model (Campbell et al. 2018) by asking them to comment on and to interrogate not only their family photos but also our own; the children then reflected on the process of working with the photos.

For six weeks in the spring of 2016, the children brought both print and digital family photos to school and engaged in various types of inquiry about them. The families were offered multiple options for sharing their photos; children who did not participate in the research study could still participate in the family photo project as class members. Together, researchers, teacher, and students discussed a range of family photos that we gathered for sharing, and we and the classroom teacher also shared our own family photos and answered the children's questions about them. Engaging in various forms of storytelling and inquiry, the children talked in pairs, using art materials to manipulate black-and-white enlargements of their family photos and iPad apps to create collages and making audio recordings of their families' stories and about their inquiry and art-making processes.

In a culminating event, parents and other children in the school viewed the research study children's various family stories, which were displayed in the form of printed digital posters, handmade paper collages, and audio recordings in which the children explained their work, and viewers could listen and ask questions. And the children were each interviewed to share their insights both about their family photos and about the research as a whole.

Our research entailed a blending of ethnography with phenomenology to capture the essence of the children's experience and to look closely at how their bodies and senses interacted with technologies (Enriquez et al. 2016; Merleau-Ponty [1945] 1962; [1948] 2004). To assess the lived, tacit features of both the photo work and the classroom moments between students and adults, we included an account of the children's affective flows and the ways that the literacy work was registered on their bodies (Massumi 2011).

We found that, as they used iPads, there were flows and intensities of emotions both when they shared their visuals and laughed together and when they were quiet and contemplative about the family collages. The strong relational feel to their visual work resulted in the significantly remixed practices we describe in the next section. We took detailed ethnographic field notes (Heath and Street with Mills 2008), interviewed the children, coproduced multimodal texts with them, and engaged in many conversations. And, applying work from the areas of affect (Ehret 2018a, 2018b), posthumanism (Kuby and Gutshall Rucker 2016), and New Literacy Studies and multimodality (Vasudevan 2011), we analyzed the data together.

PRODUCING KNOWLEDGE THROUGH EVERYDAY CULTURE

Looking at what our study schoolchildren did with digital and printed photos, art materials, and iPads led us to think about how discourses, ideologies, and narratives about families circulate and materialize in texts. We found the final multimodal text to be an important site for interrogation, but, perhaps more important, we also found that what happened along the way, from draft to draft, from medium to medium, and from person to person, offered new insights and findings about how children produce knowledge through everyday culture.

Though our analysis does not focus explicitly on social class, it is very much in the background of our interpretations of findings. Thus we have both read and drawn significantly from the works of Deborah Hicks, Anne Haas Dyson, and Pippa Stein on the practices of white and racially diverse working-class children and, specifically, on how these children improvise on their identities and think through texts.

In her study of Appalachian white working-class children, Hicks (2002) describes how hidden injuries shape the literacy trajectories of the working-class girls she studied. Dyson's work (2003) shows how the remix by very young working-class children of popular culture influences on their beginning writing reframes the value of seeing the permeable boundaries of home and school literacy practices. And, in her study of racially diverse working-class children in South Africa, Stein (2008) shows how modes come together as semiotic signifiers, much like the sections of a symphony orchestra. With notable exceptions such as the work of Susan Jones (2006), social class remains an unresearched area in the literacy literature. In particular, the literacy experiences of white working-class young people and the rich compositional and media practices they engage in are all but absent in the literature (but see Stornaiuolo and LeBlanc 2016; Thiel 2015).

Scholars have also examined how discourses, ideologies, and narratives have been materialized or "(im)materialized" across digital and nondigital spaces in ways that involve shifts in practices and subjectivities in different spaces (Burnett, Merchant, et al. 2014). Posthuman and new materialist thinking about what multimodal writing can be allows for nonrepresentational, playful understandings of how "writers" or "makers" work with nonhuman materials (Harwood and Collier 2017; Kuby and Gutshall Rucker 2016; Kuby, Spector, and Thiel 2018; Thiel 2015). Departing from a prior focus on meaning making, this work is involved in the chasing of trajectories, interrelations, and possibilities; it calls on researchers to "unknow" through visual and digital work and to adopt a living literacies approach that encourages more modes in play during literacy teaching and learning. And, in doing so, it opens up classroom spaces to alternative pedagogical models—for learning myriad possible ways of knowing and becoming through interactions with everyday texts like family photos.

REMADE AND REMIXED LITERACIES

As co-researchers, we saw that children's thinking was informed by the ways that practices moved across contexts and the ways that agency was performed relationally and materially. Family photos were an entryway into the children's inquiries about the nature of family, about producing lived pictures of their homes and their family members, and about finding how to play and be subversive with family images in creative and original ways. The theories noted above helped us capture the back and forth across the material and digitized platforms the research study children engaged with in their grade 4 space.

DEFINING REMAKING

A key aspect of our research was how the schoolchildren copied, modified, and borrowed elements and materials. Richard Dawkins (1976) introduced the notion of memes as an "evolutionary model of cultural development and change" (Knobel 2006, 411). Dawkins had three criteria for successful memes: (1) fidelity—how easily memes were copied intact and easily reproduced; (2) fecundity—for memes that were rapidly and widely replicated, distributed and attentively received; and (3) longevity—how long the memes stuck around (Knobel 2006, 413–416). Michele Knobel and Colin Lankshear (2007, 209) argue that, when talking about memes, "a concept like 'replicability' needs to include remixing as an important practice." Knobel (2006, 416) also notes how, with "cool hunting," viewers position themselves as being in the know through their early attention to particularly fertile memes, but, more important, she points to how memes affect the groups of people who take them on: "Memes are contagious patterns of cultural information that are passed from mind to mind and which directly shape and propagate key actions and mindsets of a social group" (Knobel 2006, 411). Here we look at motifs as memes and at tropes about happy families as cultural semiotic signifiers that are realized and move within and across material and digitized spaces.

During and after our research study, it was clear that there were variations in how the children responded to the family photos, in what kinds of stories they told, and in how they used materials. Some children in the classroom appeared to perform normalized pictures of their families based on common tropes and themes such as having fun and doing social things together and on classic visualizing practices such as choosing photos of their families smiling in group shots. Children who sat close to one another picked up on these tropes and recycled them, but sometimes they played with these tropes and produced different versions that included quirky, unique family traits. Some of this borrowing and playing allowed these children to represent their friendships or attachments through the remixes they produced. Other children appeared to work in a more solitary fashion, particularly when they used iPads. Figure 5.2 shows some of the research study children who are the focus of this chapter at work.

To help us think through the children's ways of knowing about families as they created and re-created family photos, we tentatively placed children in the four-quadrant graphic we devised (see figure 5.3). Our graphic was not meant to represent the complete diversity of the children's ways of working, thinking, or making, nor were its categories meant to be

Figure 5.2
Children making and remaking

static or exclusive, but only to momentarily identify the children's ways of working, which might not be consistent over time or space. Where children were finally placed in the grid could have implications for their literacy practices and the expectations placed on them at school.

For the graphic in figure 5.3, we chose four categories we derived from our observations and analyses of the children working. "Solitary" indicates practices where makers do not seem greatly influenced by the examples of others around them, nor by the adults in the room. Their productions and processes appear singular and idiosyncratic. "Relational" indicates practices where the children seem to borrow from other children's ideas and tropes about families and materials that reflect their friendships with and sometimes admiration of those they borrow from. The two categories in the lower level of the graphic refer to which kinds of stories the children tell about their families and how the children use materials. "Subversive/Independent" refers to when the children's stories and use of materials defy or depart from conventional school practices and expectations for stories about families. "Sanctioned/Performative" refers to when the children's expected stories about happy families are performed in conventional ways, such as writing or using explanatory captions.

Using their self-chosen pseudonyms, we tentatively placed Poop, Billy Bob ("Corn Cob Billy Bob" in full), Kenjii, and Ssundee near the graphic categories we thought matched how they came to know through their engagement with family photos. All four children were nine or ten years old and in the same grade 4 class at the time of our research study. Poop (solitary, relational) moved in and around the areas where the children were working. Billy Bob (relational, sanctioned/performative) and Kenjii (subversive/independent, sanctioned/performative) were close friends, often choosing to work together away from the others. And Ssundee (solitary, subversive/independent) worked on his own at his desk, but near the other children in the class.

The several digitized and material collages displayed below were produced by the study children in their classroom. Although they may appear to be final products, they were selected from among the available drafts

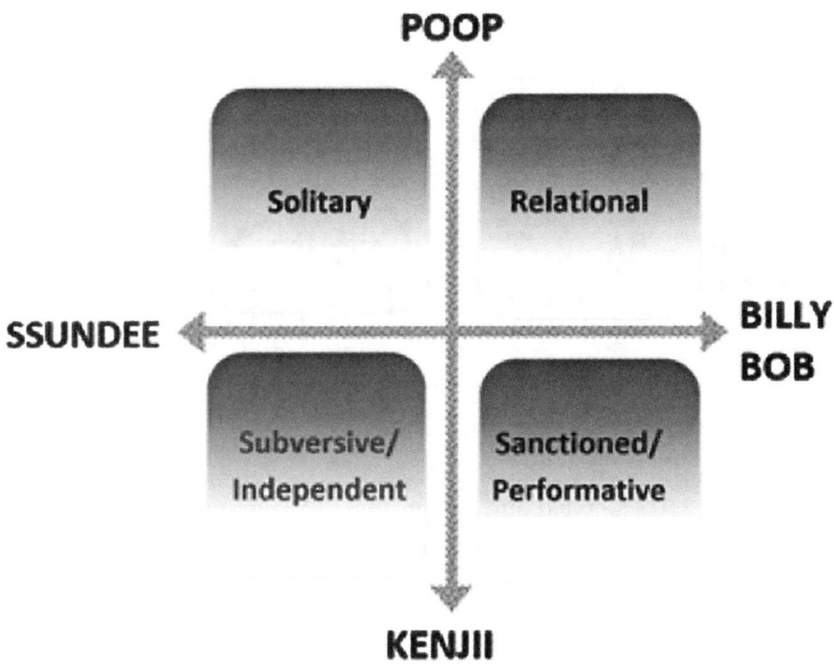

Figure 5.3
Ways of knowing and making. Design credit: D. Collier

the children made, and thus represent only a part of their final work about their families. We chose these collages because they were produced at similar points in time and showed how the study children influenced one another's work.

BILLY BOB AS RELATIONAL AND SANCTIONED/PERFORMATIVE

During his interview, Billy Bob described his family as two families blended into one, with his stepdad and stepbrother joining his mother and him, even though his stepbrother did not live with them full-time. The images in figure 5.4 (*left to right*) are

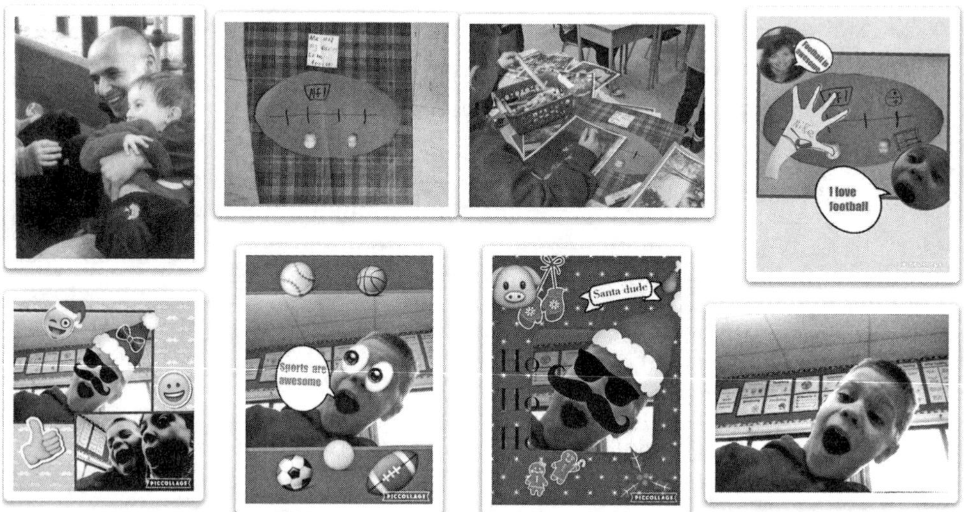

Figure 5.4
Billy Bob's material and digitized family drafts

TOP: 1. Billy Bob's stepdad and stepbrother at playground with Billy Bob (partially in photo) looking at them and them looking at him. 2. Draft of Billy Bob's collage in paper, with his and his stepbrother's faces superimposed and Post-it note where he has written "Me and my family love football." 3. Photo of Billy Bob working on that collage. 4. More elaborate collage with Billy Bob's mother in top left saying, "Football is awesome," and selfie of him at bottom right yelling, "I love football!," hand holding football with Nike watch on his wrist, number 30—Billy Bob's football jersey number—and logo for Pittsburgh Steelers football team.

BOTTOM: 1. PicCollage of Billy Bob as cool, mustached Santa, with winky and smiley emojis and thumbs-up sticker, and another selfie with another classmate, with beautiful cloudy day in background. 2. Another iteration of diagonal selfie with speech balloon "Sports are awesome" and various sports balls on green background. 3. Diagonal selfie again in cool Santa disguise with label "Santa Dude," some Christmas mitts, pig emoji, chicken drumstick, holly, and gingerbread folks with "Ho Ho Ho" down side. 4. Original surprised-face diagonal selfie upon which all others are based.

The drafts and moments captured in figure 5.4 originate from Billy Bob's playing with his friends and classmates, the iPad, and the selfie that ends up in the final collage. In this process, Billy Bob incorporated the football motif into his work and introduced it to his peers.

When explaining his featured collage (see figure 5.5) in his audio story, Billy Bob talked about all the things his family did together. He clearly wanted to show how two families came together as one in his family story. He included speech balloons and a cropped selfie that mimicked his earlier play on the iPad. As he built his collage image over time, he added key symbols like the Nike watch, the NFL acronym, and the Pittsburgh Steelers logo. He never faltered in representing his family's love of sports and enthusiasm for one another: he portrayed them as fun loving and happy with access to resources (expensive watches, football lessons, and tickets for games). The talk and stories that Billy Bob performed were thus the kinds that the teacher and researchers expected.

KENJII AS SUBVERSIVE/INDEPENDENT AND SANCTIONED/PERFORMATIVE

Kenjii was a very close friend of his classmate Billy Bob; the two of them often took pictures of each other across the room with their iPads. And,

Figure 5.5
Billy Bob's featured family collage

when given permission during the family photo study project, they would sit together, apart from the others at the back of the classroom. It is important to note that Kenjii only brought in one family photo for this project; other children brought in anywhere from three to twenty photos. In figures 5.6 and 5.7 are some representative samples of what Kenjii produced in material, digitized, and hybrid forms during the month-long period of working with family photos.

As he worked with his photo and materials over time, Kenjii made playful changes on his iPad, borrowing bits and ideas to illustrate his family, which he described as "fun." And, as he did so, his own ideas about family moved from serious to silly. The images in figure 5.6 (*left to right*) are

Figure 5.6
Kenjii's material and digitized family drafts

TOP: 1. Kenjii's original family photo depicts time when he and his family (mother, father, twin siblings, and Kenjii, *center*) visited Epcot Center in Disneyland. (Note matching outfits of children.) 2. Kenjii transforms his family into pirates and bandits with silhouette of TIE fighter (spacecraft from *Star Wars*) in background. 3. Kenjii transforms his family to more-bearded (Duck Dynasty?) and less-threatening group. 4. Kenjii is more fully elaborated in technicolor in center.

BOTTOM: 1. This one of hundreds of selfies Kenjii took and shared with his friends during study project mimics selfie taken by Billy Bob displayed in BOTTOM panel 4 of figure 5.4. 2. Using iPad, Kenjii photographs his family photo and includes more predictable caption: "I love my family." 3. Toward end of study project, Kenjii used PicCollage to create a written version of his family trip story, shared with us earlier on to explain why this family photo was important and why he had so few family photos. The trip occurred soon after his baby brother had recovered from surgery, and Kenjii explained that his family did not want photos of the hospital or of his brother hooked up to tubes. To tell the story of his baby brother's illness and recovery, he used snipping tool in PicCollage to cut out his brother's picture and place it, as if in incubator, at bottom of page; 4. Like many other children in his class, Kenjii created a collage that used his family photo and sports images, with captions about his family's "coolness."

Kenjii often played around with unsanctioned and exploratory ways of knowing through his family photography inquiries. His early doodling on versions of his family photo playfully contradicted the directions of those adults in the room who were concerned at first about how children might "deface" their family photos. The winding and indirect ways in which children like Kenjii got around to telling family stories also sometimes caused some discomfort among the adults in the room and subverted linear classroom norms about "how things get done." Although Kenjii crossed the lines of what kind of work and stories were expected, he also produced some conventional representations, such as those in TOP panels in figure 5.6, like Billy Bob's in TOP panel 1 of figure 5.4, as well as powerful family stories such as "My family story" in BOTTOM panel 3 of figure 5.6.

Like other classmate participants, Kenjii explored a great deal during this arts inquiry process. Often working with Billy Bob and following his lead (see figure 5.5), Kenjii decided to feature the collage shown in figure 5.7 in his final presentation to parents and schoolmates. Building on Billy Bob's inclusion of a football in his collage, Kenjii placed a baseball in the center of his, with the heads of all his family members on top of it. And Kenjii did indeed regularly play baseball and attend baseball games with his family, just as Billy Bob played football and attended football games with his. Kenjii's energy and playfulness are apparent in the items he included in his collage; in the crown on which he wrote "Lilly's the Queen" and in the yellow, orange, and blue squares he labeled as "confetti," explaining on a Post-it, "I put confetti because my house is a party." Whether Kenjii placed the confetti squares in the collage because they looked good or just because he felt like it is unclear. His consistent message of family love is reinforced by the message "L♥VE U GUYS." At one point, Kenjii told us he included leaves because his family collected

Figure 5.7
Kenjii's featured family collage

leaves, but said he did not know why he also included tree bark. It seems that some of these materials must just have felt or seemed right. Finally, Kenjii included a golden retriever, cut out from some wallpaper found by an educational assistant for the class, to represent "My Dog Carly," and he added a stick in the dog's mouth.

Though often subversive or unsanctioned, Kenjii's ways of knowing were sometimes sanctioned, too, as noted above, because they were also relational—through his connections with Billy Bob and his appropriation and remaking of Billy Bob's images and ideas. And though there is some divergence between Kenjii's family stories and the kinds of things he felt compelled to include in his artwork, there is also much resonance between them.

POOP AS SOLITARY AND RELATIONAL

Poop was interested in using materials and iPads to express stories about her family. On a modified academic program, she often worked around the periphery of the social groups in the classroom. And when she did work or sit with another student, the teacher tended to be the one initiating and facilitating the partnership. Poop brought to school photos of her mother and stepdad and her sightseeing at Niagara Falls and at a local event, as well as several photos of her alone with her biological father, whom she was only able to see periodically.

The images in figure 5.8 (*left to right*) are

Figure 5.8
Poop's material and digitized family drafts

TOP: 1. Family photo Poop used for very first story she told or made about her family, taken at Niagara Falls in front of fabricated Niagara Falls. She has added surprised circular mouths on her family members' faces, swirling blue for water of falls, and she has her mother and herself yelling, "Help Me," and her stepfather yelling, "Help us," in speech balloons. 2. In second version, starting from same black-and-white photo, Poop has added pop-up feature, using purple foam heart provided by teacher; this idea was borrowed from the girl sitting near Poop who had created a similar pop-up feature. (When asked, Poop insisted that it was her own idea.) On purple heart, she has written "Look" above and "Open" below the keyhole she has drawn on the heart. 3. In third image, Poop has made PicCollage that repeats image of her stepfather, and then included full collage of her other family members, representing everyone she considered part of her family.

BOTTOM: 1. In first image, Poop plays with PicCollage app by spiraling images in diminishing size around cropped image from her paper version, which again draws eye to Poop and her stepfather looking at her. 2. In next collage, she plays again with her various images in a more random fashion. 3. Final image, which includes digital collage of each of her story collages, displayed in what appears to be more balanced fashion, represents, Poop told us simply, "my family."

For Poop's featured family collage (see figure 5.9), she created a football, placed on top of pinecone-patterned wallpaper. Like Billy Bob and

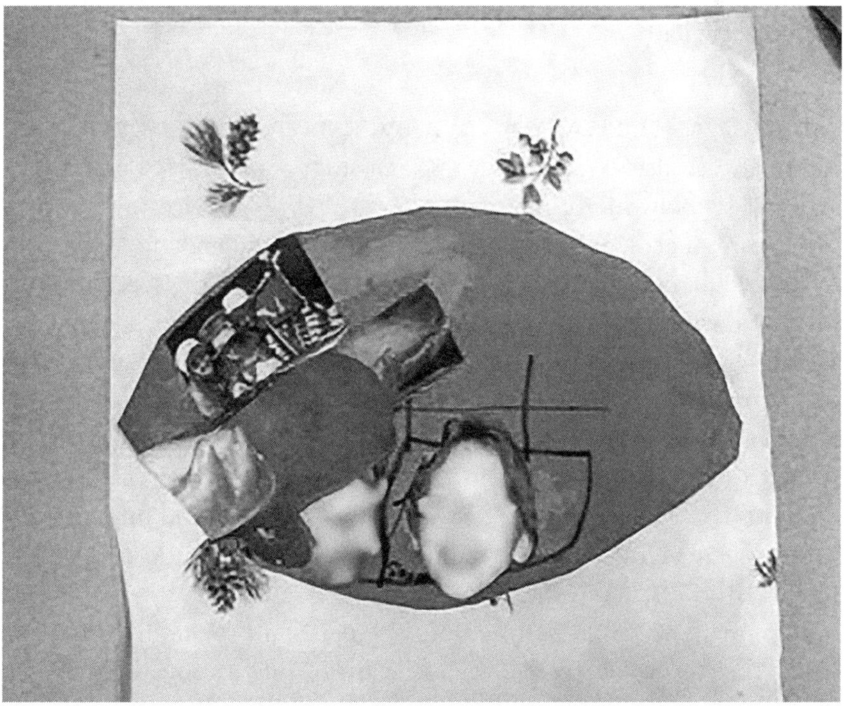

Figure 5.9
Poop's featured family collage

Kenjii, she chose a sports ball as centerpiece for her family members. And, also like Billy Bob and Kenjii, she deconstructed family photos to superimpose images of her family members on this sports image. For her featured collage, Poop borrowed the idea of closeness that the football image represents, even though it diverged from her actual family story. (But again, when asked, Poop insisted that the football was her own idea—and also that she and her stepfather liked to play football.) Almost as an afterthought, Poop included an image of her mother and stepfather in a theme park at the upper left edge of her football.

Poop may have borrowed the football image to show family cohesion or her desire for a family that plays football, or she may have included the image simply because it appealed to her. Poop had no access to class discourses or to middle-class resources or practices. Her work was both solitary—she worked with no other child, yet borrowed others' resources—and relational in the way that she highly valued family members, especially her stepfather.

SSUNDEE AS SOLITARY AND SUBVERSIVE/INDEPENDENT

Although Ssundee's work in our research study was always solitary—like all of his schoolwork for that matter—and always appeared to follow his own desires, needs, and particular ways of doing and making, he seemed to enjoy much of the work he did using materials and digital tools. During math, when other students were working on paper-and-pencil tasks, Ssundee often worked in 3-D; his pockets were filled with an assortment of unusual objects: little paper maps, bacon-printed duct tape, various fasteners, and other small objects. Though not confrontational, he found it hard to follow directions and to produce written work. His personal interests—in Minecraft, Minecraft YouTube videos, and other video games—were highly developed, and he was eager to tell others, especially interested adults, about them.

Layering, collecting, and humor were persistent themes in Ssundee's work. The images of figure 5.10 (*left to right*) show various examples of his making:

Figure 5.10
Ssundee's material and digitized family drafts

TOP: 1. In photo showing his intense concentration and pleasure when working on items like this, Ssundee is creating smoke for his construction-paper train out of paper and tape. 2. Pictured here are his brother (*left*), Ssundee, and his friend (*right*). From their T-shirts in this black-and-white printout of his family photo, Ssundee has removed logos to use as stickers or emojis in another place. 3. Sometimes wary of having his picture taken and declining to be recorded on video, Ssundee did play with some selfies he took, though they often showed only part of his face, like this one. 4. Photo of Ssundee's arm, which he took and reused in other collages.

BOTTOM: 1. Here Ssundee has laid six photos, all taken at the same Christmas event, on his desk and photographed them. 2. He has then imported this image into PicCollage and added layers of stickers and emojis in columns and rows. 3. Experimenting further, Ssundee has layered stickers and emojis on photo of his own arm and added PicCollage logo as well as larger smiley emoji, with bow tie, which he appears to be reaching for. 4. and 5. Ssundee experiments still further in these last two images with zooming in on and reorienting his emoji row. No one else in his class played with stickers and emojis in this way; Ssundee's solitary process only tangentially aligned with normative expectations around family photos and family stories.

Figure 5.11
Ssundee's featured family collage

In Ssundee's featured collage (see figure 5.11), there is a 3-D story that connects to his response to materials and their potential for creating something new. He told us that the curly bit of paper was the "fire from train," whose passengers were his brother and a "random stranger" (although the stranger was, in reality, his best friend), along with a moose and his "golden retriever pet" (both cut out of wallpaper). Even though Ssundee had no such pet, it was the only element of his collage that connected him to the other study children, some of whom also included this cutout retriever in their collages.

Ssundee placed buttons he found in his pocket on the train as wheels, but covered them with masking tape so that only he knew the wheels were there. When the character standing outside of the train asks, "Can I come in pliz I will give you 10$?" the brother in the train says, "No!"

Ssundee always engaged with our research study on his own terms, and his "outputs" reflected this. He borrowed the name he chose for his pseudonym from a Minecraft video maker. In some ways, Ssundee, like Poop, falls outside expected classroom or school discourses; and like his other classmates, he had no access to (or chose to ignore) middle-class discourses about families. Though we all could see great worth in Ssundee's imagination, focus, and 3-D skills, we found it hard to see how he might transform these into practices and texts that would be valued at his school.

CONNECTING THE RESEARCH TO A LIVING LITERACIES APPROACH

Tracing memes and tropes elucidates how the schoolchildren in our study collaborated, thought, and remixed texts in new and original ways and through different modalities. "Visualizing Families" had an ethical stance to it insofar as we both sought to help children find their own voices during the research process: we wanted very much for them to make their own decisions in choosing their own pseudonyms, which of their unique family photos to bring in and which family members to foreground in them, as well as how to remix and mediate the photos. Celebrating the singularity of people, a living literacies approach is about living life on our own terms and recognizing beauty in the seemingly mundane.

A crucial element of "living life on our own terms" involves choosing our own communities of practice and peer groups. The schoolchildren who took part in our research study sometimes engaged in relational work, creating semiotic chains (Siegel 2006). Their relational work calls for researchers to think about how children's interrelations, affordances of particular tools and modes, and energy in playing with sometimes digitized materials might produce something new.

Over the course of our "Visualizing Families" project, we identified and discussed children who instigated and drove memes and multimodal compositions and who remixed texts. Not surprisingly, many of these same children were "invisible" during their official and traditional schoolwork. Becoming leaders and drivers of meaning allowed them to share their family stories and to proudly exhibit their digital and non-digital compositions and prowess. The children's engagement in playful inquiry with their family photos allowed them to explore the stories, relations, and connections that the photos suggested and to value a range of understandings about what constitutes a family. We were particularly aware of how low-income or working-class children are often positioned as users or consumers, rather than as producers, of digital tools and texts (Dolan 2016) and are often schooled in ways that focus on traditional basic skills. Providing current technologies and apps, as well as arts and crafts materials, opened up multimodal worlds for them to think and invited them to embark on new repertoires of practice.

Three of the main goals of our research were to both illustrate and disrupt conceptions of families and family photographs, to take an anthropological approach to children's making and remaking, and to question how we are all implicated when acknowledging only sanctioned ways of knowing. We contend that arts inquiry with family photos that move across material and digitized spaces illuminates pathways, relationships, connections, and disjunctions between students and literacy practices. Thinking through solitary, relational, sanctioned, and subversive ways of knowing helps us support children as they tell their diverse, complex family stories and as they express ideas that may exceed and even subvert normative sociocultural conceptions of what constitutes a family. Our research suggests that classrooms can indeed become more accepting spaces where children can tell their lived family stories without fear of judgment or embarrassment. All families are unique, and visualizing this uniqueness in playful and imaginative ways allows children to think and learn on their own terms.

CONCLUSION

"Knowing," as presented through our family photos project, has to do with getting inside the logic of a mode, thinking through that mode, and thinking across other genres of texts. What stands out as a model for knowing and thinking is the way that Ssundee, Poop, Kenji, and Billy Bob improvised with their family photos and made them distinctive through multimodal and semiotic tools such as emojis or varied materials like little bits of paper taped on with duct tape. Sometimes their thinking during compositional practices involved nondigital texts like arts and crafts materials; at other times, it involved working with digital apps like PicCollage or watching YouTube videos to get instructions on how to make something.

This formulation of thinking and knowing entailed the deliberate "unknowing" (Vasudevan 2011) of schooled ways of thinking (e.g., doing paired reading or filling in blanks). The children who participated in our research study instead privileged visuals, icons, and written text. At times, the shape, color, and texture of a composition were crucial, such as when the children made use of the old-fashioned wallpaper on the crafts table; at other times, experiencing and knowing (Ehret 2018a) came through superimposing an icon or emoji on top of a visual. What is significant here is that, by closely observing children and charting or mapping out their choices, decisions, revisions, struggles, questions, and moments of teché leading to wonderment (Delagrange 2011), researchers can bring newer ways of knowing to the surface. Throughout *Living Literacies*, these newer ways of knowing rely heavily on the idiosyncratic ways people live their lives and engage in habits of mind and heart that are so frequently unseen or overlooked within official, formal contexts and normative ideologies and discourses.

Figure 6.1
Giant's footprint

6

CREATING: A LIVING LITERACIES APPROACH

Kate Pahl, Steve Pool, and Zanib Rasool

The world of change is made of self-creative expression.
—Brian Massumi (2011, 21)

CREATIVITY AND LITERACY

This chapter explores the flow between creativity and literacy to learn what we can from their connection and, in doing so, to consider what it is about literacy that can be reimagined. From the perspective of living literacies, we understand that creativity is present at all points in the process of generating meaning and that literacy is inherently multimodal: its ideas can "seep" from talk to writing to drawing. Gunther Kress (1997) used the term "transduction" to describe how ideas move across modes. And, as Ruth Finnegan (2015, 136) tells us, in the movement from performance to text and others, "overtones from one form of realization seep into others." Multimodality is full of transformations (Pahl 1999). The idea of multimodality requires us to unsettle and reconsider how literacy and language are currently defined—and to imagine what both could be.

Creativity is a key ingredient in how we story our worlds. The word "creativity" is used here in its widest sense to refer to the making of anything new, to include both the material and the (im)material—a thing, an idea, or a moment (Burnett, Merchant, et al. 2014). Creative approaches include multimodal meaning making and remaking in a process of transformation, drawing on multiple histories of practice from across the creative arts.

Understood as a "potentially unmade space," literacy becomes about the unfolding moment when something connected to literacy happens. The literacy event requires creativity to act; the creation of something new that flows in and out of meaning reinvigorates literacy and opens new territories—it becomes alive with the possibility of what is to come. To break it free from its traditional moorings, however, requires a leap of creative thought and a change in what we consider to be the uses of literacy. And this leap requires an understanding of the ways in which the complex relations of everyday life animate literacy events as they are forming (Pahl 2014a).

The literacy event is a living production of meaning that can be written and read, inscribed and interpreted; creativity allows for it to be remade in the moment. Creativity can refer to new meanings or new modes of communication to produce new definitions of what literacy can be. Within education more generally, researchers Pamela Burnard, Anna Craft, and colleagues (2006) have used the term "possibility thinking" to suggest an innovative, relevant, and meaningful process that includes expanded creative thinking.

We use the concept of creativity to expand the definition of literacy—to enable it to live in the everyday world, linking it to a transformative process. By this, we mean a living production of meaning that is open to be both written and read, inscribed and interpreted. Within literacy studies, literacy can refer to new meanings, new modes of communication, or new definitions of what it can be (Mavers 2011); within education more generally, it can refer to how children develop their own ideas and explore further possibilities (Craft 2002). Creativity as transformative meaning making can open up new stories and reveal cultural spaces of difference and disruption.

Both literacy and creativity emerge within everyday common cultures, entwined with visual and multimodal ways of seeing and reading the world (Boggs, Duarte, and Manglitz 2017). In this chapter, Kate Pahl and Steve Pool describe their shared work in schools and communities, and scholar activist Zanib Rasool describes a project involving an artist working with women's intergenerational stories. The chapter ends by considering how creativity and literacy can be rethought in relation to each other.

THE LITERACY EVENT AS A CREATIVE ACT

Kate Pahl and Steve Pool

When the literacy event is understood as a creative act, the world becomes rich in multiplicities of meanings, readings, and writings. Here we and our source authors ask a number of "What if ... ?" questions that challenge our current, traditional definitions of literacy. In doing so, we aim to create a space where literacy can become more than it is now—in new, dynamic and relevant ways. Thus Kevin Leander and Gail Boldt (2013, 41) ask us: "What might we make of the invitation to consider literacy in 'and ... and ... and' relations?"

We start with the everyday literacy event, an act that could include inscription, oral stories, multimodal meaning making or writing where literacy plays a role (Barton 1994, 36). This "What if ... ?" approach enables researchers to resituate literacy events as being about something beyond literacy as currently defined, to rethink and reconsider literacy as something new perhaps. By looking at the literacy event as a creative act, as the making of something new that is embedded within, and relates to, a complex weave of space, intention, and affect, we can begin to understand literacy differently, and, by connecting it to questions of emergence and of process, we can explore how literacy emerges, where it goes, and what it could be. A living literacies approach considers method as well as theory, which opens out a methodological inquiry: How can literacy be reconceptualized? What happens when we consider literacy as a creative "event"?

To do this, we are helped by insights from Christian Ehret, who, drawing on Brian Massumi's ideas (2011) about the "coming-into-being" of the literacy event, described it as "the singular, amodal feeling of something happening produced through emergent relations between bodies, human and nonhuman" (Ehret 2018b, 564). We should *feel* literacy through the literacy event, Ehret tells us, and we should consider the event as propositional—an "as if" moment in time. This would allow us to understand it as a series of interrelations that could include creative acts of reading and writing and actively generating new meanings more fully entwined with the materiality of the world. When we think about the "What if ... ?" nature of literacy, the idea of the literacy event as a creative act comes into play. A creative act can be disruptive: creativity emerges from complex, chaotic conditions into more recognizable forms. But this process of forming is opaque, argues Brian Massumi (2011), whose ideas enable us to theorize toward an expansive view of literacy—*prior* to the act of inscription and connected to ideas of becoming and emergence.

This chapter explores the literacy event as it moves away from the binary constructions—the divides between oral and written text and between visual, gestural, and haptic modes, for example—that can dominate literacy pedagogies. Moments when meaning is made can open out into a broader understanding of the literacy event in all its multiplicity. Thus an image of a dance can include both written text and the literacy event as a creative act in a wider landscape of communication. Literacy is part of a moving web of complex practices. Thinking about literacy through the literacy event allows us to move literacy beyond the construction of abstract meaning and place it back in the world of feeling and affect (Ehret 2018b).

In *Before Writing*, Kress (1997) identified how young children moved quite seamlessly between writing and drawing. An example of this would be when a child began to write a letter "B," but drew a baby image, with a small eye and face nested inside the "B." The letter "B" was also the first letter of the child's name. But the moment of marking a very small part of the process of mark making the "B" baby sign. As Cathy Burnett and Guy Merchant (2018, 8) observe, the semiosis is ongoing; it "emphasizes the process of making meaning as part of life." Viewing literacy as an open process entwined with life makes it different from fixed ideas of where we find meaning.

Seeing the literacy event as boundless and free from edges, we describe the moments of significance that become literacy events where we align as artist and as researcher. Experienced in discussions or written in field notes, and held in memory, these moments sit in a sea of talk and gesture. And though they are written or articulated in formal ways into children's jotters, research articles, films, and presentations, we find it useful here to speculate about how the literacy events they give rise to are held within bodies, feelings, movements, and memories. In doing so, our literacy research becomes more about "the relations mediated through the process of making meaning" (Burnett and Merchant 2018, 8).

In the "ninja" research study discussed below (see "Language as Talisman" under "Chapter 6 Featured Studies" in appendix), a group of boys made a film about a world without language (Escott and Pahl 2017), but where a "talking permit" could be used to give the group's "ninjas" permission to talk. And though the writing of the talking permit was fixed, swirling around it were actions, gestures, creative play, and language. The currents of the everyday shift and move across the literacy event, shaping and then moving it along into a different propositional space. Seeing the creative literacy act as a literacy event amplifies the "new-ness" of literacy as a mode of communication, its, "coming into its new-ness out of the soon to be prior background activity it will have left creatively behind" (Massumi 2011, 3).

Literate behavior involves the emergence of writing, gesture, speech, inscription, and mark making. It could include a chalk drawing on a sidewalk, a sudden movement to indicate a letter on a page, or a text message on a smartphone. Shirley Brice Heath (1983, 50) defined "literacy event" as "any occasion in which a piece of writing is integral to the nature of the participants' interactions and their interpretive processes." The literacy event takes place in time and space, and can be observed: a person can write a shopping list or inscribe a note on a piece of paper, a child can make a drawing and add a letter or two to that drawing.

Massumi (2011) sees the literacy event as a fleeting intervention in the world, situated inside an ongoing process of feeling, becoming, and relating, an intervention that helps us imagine change in movement as held within the fabric of the everyday. But to understand the felt nature of the literacy event requires new practices of recognition—practices that can be shared, co-felt, and coproduced. Creating involves feeling: as a child inscribes, the child also feels that moment, which arises from a position of multiplicity in the process of becoming (Beck and Gleyzon 2016).

In the sections to follow, we work through creative acts and literacy events in the context of our research study projects (see appendix). And though our work involves complex webs of thoughts and interconnections, we have tried our best not to oversimplify them or to isolate specific moments just to stress a point. We hope that our readers will create their own meanings and relations within the stories we present and that unfolding the relational moments of the literacy event will make the relationship between creativity and literacy more knowable and visible. A creative approach to the literacy event offers a felt and embodied way in to thinking about literacy, one that considers possibilities and furtherness and that opens the way to "new-ness." Seeing the literacy event in this way creates a new kind of feeling about its event-ness: "It is because an event 'enjoys itself' in this arcingly immediate way that it is able to follow through with itself. And it is because it follows through with *itself* that it qualifies as self-creative" (Massumi 2011, 4).

RESEARCHING CREATIVE LITERACIES

Over a period of ten years, the two of us have collaborated on research study projects involving artists working in schools. In exploring how schoolchildren made meaning in different ways, literacy became a collecting thread within their meaning making, as it expanded and contracted across multiple modalities.

On one such study project, "A Reason to Write" (see appendix) artists worked with the children to explore their reasons for writing; in doing so, they experimented with different forms of writing. One morning, the children came into the classroom to discover that one of the artists had strewn giant objects made of white paper in their path—a teacup, a shoe, and a giant foot. The children were invited to discuss these objects, then encouraged by the teacher to take them outside and to trace their outlines in chalk on the playground tarmac. We observed how writing became a form of inscription that could involve tracing a giant's footprint in chalk (see figure 6.1 at start of chapter).

Our research participants included six children, aged 10–11, who worked with artists to explore moments of creativity within their school, drawing on film, still images, and field notes as data (Pahl and Pool 2011). Searching for a moment from the data that would help them explain their thoughts, they chose a moment when a boy who called himself "Declan" was photographed dancing in the school hall, with the letters "A-C-H-I-E-V-E-M-E-N-T" displayed above him and the branches of a tree drawn on the wall behind him appearing to grow from the top of his head—and with darkened eyebrows, a mustache, and a goatee added to his image to preserve his anonymity (see figure 6.2).

Figure 6.2
Declan dancing

The photograph of Declan dancing as a form of inscription lay in the moment, fleeting and ephemeral, highlighted later as being significant in an analytic discussion with the children. In the project episodes, the literacy event, the writing, and the photographic act became creative. As an interruption and a provocation, the literacy event here was an open cycle of inscription and interpretation. For the children present when the original image of Declan dancing was taken, the photograph captures a moment of transgression; it articulates a "between space" of laughter, of breaking out, a moment outside any formal teaching or learning structure, which the children would later (after the photo "additions" were made) describe as "messing about" (Pahl and Pool 2011).

The photograph became the symbol of how this "messing about" inscribed itself into the world through the original movement, the capturing of it, the conversations around it, and the additions made to it. The literacy event was located in a broader space of collective meaning making. Made playful by the juxtaposition of the message "ACHIEVEMENT" and the dance, and provided with a new meaning when the darkened eyebrows, mustache, and goatee were added to preserve Declan's anonymity, the image is also not so much about language as it is about the importance of creative "messing about" in school—whose meaning traveled, and moved on.

We learned that the schoolchildren valued space that was not structured and, perhaps more important, that they viewed any structure, however open, creative, or artistic, not as "messing about," but simply as schoolwork. The children helped us see that what we considered free and open artistic play sat within a structure that was, for them, all too familiar and restrictive.

Researching creative literacies calls for an expansive multimodal, material, and auditory concept of literacy, one that no longer sees language as monomodal but instead acknowledges that the visual, gestural, and oral aspects of language let in much more meaning than written words alone (Maybin 2013). Multimodality offers a way to see literacy as part of a wider landscape of meaning making. Multimodal scholarship involves watching children's meaning making very closely. Moments of transformation within everyday text making are often connected to transmodal shifts, as something described in an oral story becomes reworked and retold within both an image and writing together (Pahl 1999).

The work of Gunther Kress (1997) and Diane Mavers (2011) has helped us understand how children transform the materials around them in moments of meaning making. Although simple activities such as copying, tracing, or etching onto a surface can appear to be quite dull, the process of inscription itself can lead to new and complex creative opportunities, as the image in figure 6.2 illustrates. The ordinary, Mavers (2011, 1) tells us, can become extraordinary and the unremarkable remarkable. Thus, in the expansion of meaning in the photo of Declan dancing, wider connective threads are pulled in: the word "ACHIEVEMENT" above him signifies something about what school is, and the felt experience of dancing produces a feeling of joy and momentary escape from the structures of school. The expansion of meaning in the moment when meaning becomes multimodal, material, and embodied makes literacy different and more fluid, and its transitory nature comes into focus.

CREATIVE INTERRUPTIONS AND DISRUPTIONS

What would a world without language look like? Our work has involved creating opportunities for schoolchildren to imagine this. In "Language as Talisman" (see appendix), this involved making films that evoked a battlefield of objects wielded by angry ninjas who used force in a world without language where talking was banned. The only way to speak was to get a "talking permit," and language was conceptualized as an object that could become granted through this mechanism (Escott and Pahl 2017).

In this play-fight project episode, most of the interactions were without language. The talking permit became the focal point of meaning in the assemblage that was the playground, where the ways in which language was constructed could be unfolded, then folded back together in a new creative moment, involving objects—play swords, a talking permit, and a bench—that themselves disturbed moments of linguistic meaning making (Escott and Pahl 2017).

Making objects the focus of research can disturb linguistic certainties, and these material orientations can themselves disturb and disrupt settled patterns of speaking and writing. The films made in this episode contain an element of surprise. The decisions to jump, to use the swords, to create the drama arose in moments of relational action between the schoolchildren, and the creativity of those decision became enmeshed in complex material multimodal practices that included the use of gestures, writing, speech, and material objects. To understand the meanings that the children produced, we had to take into account all of these (Escott and Pahl 2017).

Our work in community contexts has enabled us to come close to moments of creativity, where literacies are threaded through with moments, ideas, and acts of possibility. Celebrating the "What if ... ?" in creative action, possibility thinking (Burnard et al. 2006) gives rise to moments of disruption that create their own arcs of making. These sometimes fleeting "creative interruptions" can take many forms. They can become gestures, shouts, inscriptions, poems, sounds, films, books, images, or scores. Our work has explored the questions of what happens when we see the creative act as part of a larger literacy event. At what points are reading, writing, and communicative exchanges happening? And how are these points held within the concept of the literacy event?

CREATIVITY AS ODD AND STRANGE

Our "Odd: Feeling Different in the World of Education" project, where multimodal approaches to expressing an idea were coproduced across a research community, asked schoolchildren to research what it means to feel odd in school (see appendix). We instantiated creativity in what we called an "Odd Box" (see figure 6.3), an empty box Steve gave the children, asking each of the classes to fill it with unusual, unfamiliar, and strange stuff. And when they did, they produced strange and wonderful ideas that helped us all think what "odd" could mean.

The moment when a creative act happens can be a moment of surprise (Nelson, Hull, and Young 2013). Here the surprise was located in

Figure 6.3
"Odd Box"

the everyday. Effective surprises are not special or rarefied, but everyday kinds of occurrences. They have the quality of obviousness about them, producing a shock of recognition when people discover the unexpected within them (Nelson, Hull, and Young 2013). The surprise works for a literacy event—its moment of strangeness becomes discovered anew in words. In our work in schools, our project team used "What if … ?" as an invitational moment: What if we were all odd? What if we could all have a superpower? This then led to the impelling need to create, to act—and within the act of creating lay the moment of the literacy event.

Our work has explored how schoolchildren combine words with images, gestures, sounds, feelings, inscriptions on the body, and dancing (Pool and Pahl 2015). The literacy event is a moment of coming together (Nelson, Hull, and Young 2013). Its mixture of modes can look messy but has a purposefulness about it that is creative (Kress 1997). The event opens up a space in which to explore literacy as interaction and movement—as temporal and situated as well as embedded within the world. Felt and embodied, the sensory nature of the literacy event is also part of its being. Though it can be fleeting and cannot quite be held within a moment, the event nevertheless holds a wide-ranging emergent repertoire of communicative practices that include the visual, aural, gestural, and embodied modes, as well as affect and feeling (see figure 6.4)—all of which produce a creative act.

Whereas New Literacy Studies helps us see everyday events, multimodal theory opens up our seeing (Kress 1997). When we watch these multimodal moments of meaning making, we see literacy as something always in process. Creative acts likewise can be identified as happening in relational, everyday spaces. Children's pathways to literacy are entwined with an understanding of creativity as always enacted in practice, relationally, and in moment-by-moment sites of transformation. By focusing on the moment of creation in the literacy event, New Literacy Studies centers the act of creative meaning making within literacy pedagogies. Literacy is changing, and it needs to be allowed to become what people *do* with it, rather than how they perceive it or how schooling shapes it. To capture the fleeting, changing nature of literacy, we need to see literacy events as not fixed. Literacy pedagogy and research involve moving "with" children and young people to support the expansive creativities of

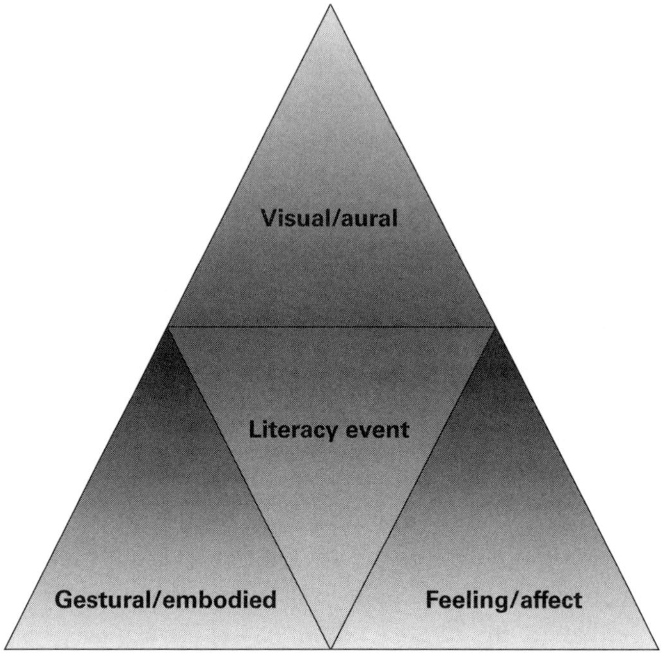

Figure 6.4
Facets of the literacy event. Created by: Kate Pahl

their meaning making and to understand the literacy event as co-felt and co-expressed (Ehret 2018b).

THE CREATIVE ACT AS TRANSFORMATIONAL

The creative arts can position young people differently, enabling them to draw on different repertoires of communicative practices (Blommaert and Backus 2012). Literacy research has used arts-based approaches to open up different kinds of modalities and literacies for young people (Pahl and Rowsell 2010).

In their research with adolescents in New York City, Lalitha Vasudevan and Tiffany DeJaynes (2013) identified when young people experienced small moments of inspiration—in jamming on a piano, for example, or in scripting a story on a New York sidewalk—that led to new conceptualizations of where their agency lay. Cultures of participation are lifted into creative acts through such moments. In their "Space2Create" project, involving young people across the globe engaging in digital authoring projects, Amy Stornaiuolo and Jin Kyeong Jung (2017, 103) found that working relationally enabled students to learn how "not just to speak *up* or speak *against* something but how to speak *with* others and speak *for* their commitments, transforming themselves and others as they participated in a 'new rhetoric of public engagement.'"

The arts can serve as a form of civic engagement, empowering young people's voices in many modes and in spaces where this is urgently needed. Many of the young people in our research projects created films to suggest ideas they could not put into more formal forms of writing. The arts can make an important contribution to the mix of educational practices by widening the scope of what can be said. Indeed, they offer a place of autonomy and resistance to dominant modes—where meaning, emotions, feelings, and desires can be articulated and communicated, produced and made different—a place for experimentation and for alternative ways of doing things.

Opening a space for the arts to be conceptualized more fully as part of lived literacies, New Literacy Studies lets us see literacy as literacy events within an expansive terrain of meaning making that allows for many forms of creative and artistic acts to unfold within temporal and spatial texts. For a literacy event to be recognized and co-felt, however, it has to be located, often within the material world. The arts are useful here in offering alternative forms whose internal logics resist the dominant forms of literacies enacted within schools and institutions. They can become an agent for future-oriented change that encourages situated, relational, and radical work; artistic creativity can become a force for inspiration and transformation for young people.

Indeed, artistic creativity opens up new spaces, from the constructed spaces of studio work to the co-inquiry spaces of dialogue (Banks and Armstrong et al. 2014). Creative acts reach out across modes, media, and communicative practice. They go to the heart of literacy understood in its most expansive sense. Or, as Glynda A. Hull and Mark Evan Nelson (2009, 200) explain: "We believe that being prepared, in both senses of being able and willing, to communicate and understand across differences in language and other modes and media for communication, in ideology, in culture and in geography is at the heart of what it means to be literate now."

To understand and communicate across differences requires a form of "imaginative vigilance" (Hull and Nelson 2009, 221) in articulating the experience of racism, for example, or the experience of being pigeon-holed into one identity. And it requires the ability to move across differences both online and offline to make sense of the world differently.

We make a distinction between creative methods and artistic approaches (Pool 2018). Whereas creative methods can include drawing, craft, and performance as ways into creating new meanings, artistic approaches, whether visual, poetic, or embodied, can infuse these meanings to locate intergenerational narratives and to capture a language of belonging together across space and time. These approaches focus on diversity and listening as a methodology. Exploring the relationship between the creative act and social cohesion is an important part of listening. Creative methods, for their part, can open up new opportunities to listen more carefully to lived experience. In the case study described below, researchers explored how listening can enhance social cohesion, and how working with stories and artistic methodologies can create a space to do that. Zanib Rasool offers a rich and deep account of one artist's vision that transformed an oral storytelling project with a focus on Muslim women's life stories.

A CASE STUDY: CREATING AS OPENING UP NEW STORIES

Zanib Rasool

"Taking Yourself Seriously" (see appendix) used artistic methodologies to gain a more meaningful and deeper insight into Muslim women's multi-layered experiences of identity and citizenship in the United Kingdom. In the glare of current narrative discourses about Muslim women in the press, the positive contribution minority ethnic women make to social, political, and economic life can become invisible This research study aimed to celebrate the lives of British Muslim women. Sharing their life stories, eight women of Pakistani heritage told of the inner strength and resilience they had found in meeting the challenges and overcoming the barriers they faced as daughters of immigrants.

ARTISTS AS WAY MARKERS WITHIN DIASPORA CONTEXTS

It was important for me to involve South Asian artists in the project since their artistic creativity comes from a vantage point intrinsically linked to their community histories and culture. Entwined within their artworks are stories and ways of knowing. Today's South Asian artists carry with them the tales of their ancestors, the stories of partition and migration told them by their elders. I worked with the visual artist Nazia Latif, who is of Pakistani heritage like me, to explore Pakistani-heritage women's narratives of migration and identity within their diaspora contexts. In a series of conversations over a six-month period, we began to tease out the key issues involved in working with artists on life story projects. Here Nazia muses on her heritage (see figure 6.5):

> Through this project, I have learned a lot about my own family, I have been talking to my mother, I have learned about my own family's art history. My mum's grandfather, his brothers and sons were architects, calligraphers, Islamic artists, interior designers of mosques and houses. We have drifted away from our art in this country, as many members of my generation in my family are lawyers, teachers, and accountants now.

Figure 6.5
"Motherland: Memories of My Childhood" by Nazia Latif

Sometimes, even today, we feel our ancestors' presence: they are walking with us across new boundaries and into new spaces. Being more in tune with emotions, spirituality, and the unknown, artists can bring the past to life and provide us with visual images of our future. They weave a splendid web of hope that both links us with our past and takes us to our future. We need artists from diverse communities to capture the fluidity and evolving nature of our lives and identities. Members of the British Pakistani community, Pnina Werbner (1990, xii) tells us, "have invested a good deal in their adopted society and are an integral part of it." Artists, poets, writers, and actors from this community can creatively illuminate the ways in which this investment takes place and the part it plays in British life, which many current government policies fail to recognize. As Pakistani-heritage Muslim women, our cultural frame of reference, our ethnicity, spirituality and faith, and our interactions and experiences with the world let us see the world through different lenses, and poetry frees us to express those different perspectives of our lived experiences; it gives rise to a mosaic of autonomous voices. Poetry also helps make sense of everyday interactions, contradictions, and conflicts. Artists can reposition community narratives and connect us to our family histories and help create a sense of belonging for our younger generation. Through arts-based practice, we are capturing individuals' unique stories across generations. "Through storytelling and counternarratives disenfranchised people(s) are provided intellectual space to 'name their own realities'" (Kumasi 2011, 211).

What follows are some of the discussions between me and Nazia, an artist who brought her own images to bear on the narratives we collected.

DISCUSSION BETWEEN ZANIB AND NAZIA

We began by talking about how artists can illuminate invisible experiences through visual images. Artists have a social responsibility to bring untold stories to life, and minority ethnic female artists are in the right place to understand the gender inequality of marginalized women.

NAZIA: These women [in the study] paved the way for women like me. It was tough for them. I like working with multimedia, collage, patterns, fabric, sketches, digital images, painting.

ZANIB: I like writing prose and poetry. My grandfather used to write on bits of paper left lying around the house. I wish I had saved those bits of papers. Sadly, we only value these things when people are no longer with us.

NAZIA: In Pakistan, art is colorful; it is bold, symmetric patterns and textiles, everyday objects, cooking pots, buses, and lorries. I am going to look at the work of South Asian artists. I love Islamic art. I am learning so much. I am experiencing my own culture; it's fascinating. I am able to look back on women's lives and their progression. Our mothers brought their culture with them and adapted their culture to fit with this country, such as fashion influences. Every woman from Pakistan was talented. We had henna artists; we had women who sewed beautifully, did embroidery, knitting. Every house had a sewing machine. Now hardly anyone has a sewing machine; we are losing creative skills. This is my history. I've been brought up in a British culture; the more I learn about my own culture through this project, the more empowered I feel.

Talking with Nazia, I realized that art is lived in Pakistan, just as literacies are lived. It is everywhere; you do not have to visit art galleries to see art, it is simply there, as Nazia said: "It's in the everyday, the beautifully decorated clay pots, the colorful buses and motortrucks, the exteriors of people's houses, the mosques." South Asian artists give voice to their community and can articulate the realities of that community through their art the everyday oppression that Muslim women face in Western society today. They are in a unique position to shine a particular light on their community and to go beneath the surface and the superficial. As Nazia told me in August 2017:

> Art and poetry help with communication; art communicates with people. It's a way of expressing emotions and feelings, visualizing sometimes hidden elements of our lives. We are not taken seriously as artists or [do not] get praised. We are good, when we do art, we face lots of barriers; I am more confident now in my art than I was when I was younger.

We are seeing a growing interest in research to capture the human experience through the arts. Artistic approaches such as drawings, paintings, and writing open a door to a different kind of conversation, a different way of knowing, and things are articulated through arts practices that might otherwise remain unsaid. Artists like Nazia have an important role to play in the movement for social cohesion. Sandra Weber (2012,

Figure 6.6
"Clifton School: Paving the Way" by Nazia Latif

5–8) has argued that images can be used when it is hard to put things into words; that images can make us pay attention to things in new ways; that they are more memorable than words alone, incorporate multiple layers, and evoke stories or questions; and that they can enhance empathy and understanding and encourage embodied knowledge to create opportunities for social cohesion. Artists can have an important role in capturing events and moments in history of the marginalized through visual narratives, through poetry and writing, through performing arts and making those invisible lives visible. Artists produce images, poems, dances that bring human narratives and meaning making to life. They interpret, understand, and make sense of life events through the images they produce; they capture the emotions of a particular moment in time and space before it is lost to us. Artists can validate the lives of their ancestors and their struggles, and be voices for their community; they can become leaders for diversity and inclusion, and they can bring us together to create social cohesion and new spaces where such cohesion can take place. Homi Bhabha (1994, 2) talks of "in between spaces" providing elaborate strategies of selfhood, innovative sites of collaboration and contestation. These more equitable "third spaces" can create new opportunities both for minority ethnic artists to grow and leave behind the colonial history of oppression and for creativity to happen. As Nazia told me, again in August 2017: "I can only speak through my artwork; my ideas are generated by my passion for artistry" (see figure 6.6).

Zanib highlights the power of creative approaches to literacy in her analysis of how an artist works with a researcher and creates new images of oral stories that can lead to wider understandings of storied selves. In this case study, artwork is intertwined with powerful meanings and stories, and the dance between literacy and creativity comes alive.

CONCLUSION

A living literacies approach to literacy is expansive both in its conceptual framing and in its potential to change lives. Creating helps us reconceptualize the literacy event as being an event that not only involves writing, but that also can open up a new space. Exploring the felt nature of the event invites a coproductive exploration of moments of possibility.

Drawing on the work of Christian Ehret (2018b) that views the literacy event as a creative act, we have explored the potential of a more felt, relational, and affective approach to literacy. We have also related this idea, which involves seeing the remarkable in the unremarkable (Mavers 2011), to shifts and transformational change. When we write, whether our fingers are dancing over our smartphones or computer tablets or laptops, scrawling our signatures on glass frames, or making notes in jotters, we create new signs (Kress 1997). This newness is always alive and open to transformation.

The pedagogical spaces for literacy can then be alive with what *could be*. Creative acts can hold open the space of the literacy event; they can disrupt the current state of things and create spaces for new meaning and new forms of communication to grow. Feeling the literacy event can lead us into nonrepresentational spaces of affect and emotion—indeed, these feelings need acknowledging as pathways to literacy (Ehret 2018b). Some of these creative moments are small and can appear insignificant. Learning to see literacy through the concept of the literacy event involves viewing it through a wide-angled lens as multimodal, gestural, and multiple in its being and outcomes (Burnett 2015). Seeing literacy as connected to just one thing can greatly hinder our understanding of what it could be. Transformational creative change can involve dialogue between ways of knowing, as divergent and oppositional views come alive in interactive ways. Threads of the everyday and common cultures need to be woven through creative approaches to literacy (Boggs, Duarte, and Manglitz 2017) so that we can listen to cultural resources from homes and communities. Zanib's work with Nazia illuminates how hidden stories from women can come alive in a set of conversations and artworks that speak not only of hardship and migration but also of success and educational achievements. Our vision here is for a more open definition of literacy, one that rests on the idea of creativity, its diversity, and its vision for the future, where creativity invites new stories, new events, and emergence to come together. By linking creativity and the literacy event, newness surprises and engages us in a rediscovery of meaning as it emerges into the world.

7

MAKING: MATERIALIZING AFFECT THROUGH MAKER LITERACIES

Jennifer Rowsell

Everyday life is a life lived on the level of surging affects, impacts suffered or barely avoided. It takes everything we have. But it also spawns a series of little somethings dreamed up in the course of things.
—Kathleen Stewart (2007, 11)

This chapter explores making as part of a living literacies approach. I argue that, rendered as a lived practice (Barrett and Bolt 2010), making emerges from being, thinking, and feeling through modes (Kress 1997; Rowsell 2013). Due to its capacity to draw people in to elicit their thoughts and emotions, making is a fundamental part of living literacy in the everyday. Although it is often associated with creativity, innovation, and technology in some form or function, this chapter argues that making is instead about acting, being together with materials, and having free rein with ideas, emotions, and motivations—and thus that it "entails something in between knowing and not knowing" (Ellsworth 2005, 17).

Whereas contemporary makerspace pedagogies and research focus less on craft (Marsh et al. 2017), there is a long tradition of making with craft and with "craft apprenticeships" (Schrock 2014). Indeed, in Nordic countries such as Iceland, where making practices are actively encouraged and embedded in the curricula, early childhood pedagogies are based on making and craft (Jónsdóttir and Gunnarsdóttir 2017). There is an overall sense of a living practice, an embodied feel to such an approach to making, associated more with *doing* than learning craft, as in touching fabric, feeling the heft and texture of materials, and holding tools (Barone and Eisner 2012).

This chapter provides an alternative framing of making and makerspaces, one that borrows from affect theory to explain how people craft and make things as a form of experiencing meaning and as part of their everyday. Maker approaches encourage collaboration and connections with others, and this relational theme comes out strongly in the chapter's research vignettes. Connecting through stuff or objects or materials that matter to people invites techné (see glossary) and incites "acts of wonderment" (Covino 1988). Synesthesia, which entails the mixing of senses as individuals interact and engage with texts, plays a key role in these lived experiences with materials and practices applied to making. Making and design work not only involve technical skills and practices but also ignite senses and feelings. Together with synesthesia, what Sandra Abrams and I have called "tacit modalities" (Abrams and Rowsell 2019) locate memories, thoughts, people, and contexts within objects and materials that can inform modal choices during making and design work (Kress 1997; Rowsell 2013). Touching a valued object or hearing a song or smelling a familiar scent evokes memories of past experiences that are felt and sensed in the present moment (Abrams and Rowsell 2019). The word "tacit" in "tacit modalities" signals the instinctual, affective nature of reacting to a mode that impinges upon the ways we make or design and that clearly has significance for the ways that people live the literacies they enact. The feelingful aspects of making and makerspace are overshadowed at times by problem solving, by science, technology, engineering, and mathematics (STEM), and by more cognitive orientations to makerspace learning. In our work together, Sandra Abrams and I have excavated the crucial role of tacit modalities in people's experiences with texts and their design practices in formal contexts like schools and more informal contexts like homes (Abrams and Rowsell 2019).

DEFINING MAKING

Official curriculum and policy documents have tended to frame making as "learning that happens best … through a process of constructing things to share with others" (Donaldson 2014, 1). There has been a clear emphasis on the thing made and not on the invisible, ephemeral processes and practices of making it. More recently, however, emerging interpretations of making have opened up design work to fluid concepts that attribute as much importance to nonrepresentation as to representation (Leander and Boldt 2013; Lewis and Tierney 2013; Ehret 2018b). And since a living literacies approach places greater emphasis on the invisible, tacit, felt, and embodied experiences of making than on what is made (Enriquez et al. 2016), in my treatment of maker perspectives, I focus more on the creative flows and intensities that underpin young people's making—that is, on the "sticky" (Ahmed 2014), affectively driven practices young people engage in and that often motivate them more so than on the concrete, visible products they make.

Paul Carter (2004) closely examines art-making processes and ways of knowing that emerge when artists make and design things. He explores not only how the decisions made during making are material ones, but also how "a good *techné,* or craft of shaping or combination, has to be open to criticism and correction" (Carter 2004, xi). Making therefore draws on the matter and practices involved in good design work, which Carter (2004) sees as experiential, haptic, performative, and embodied, although Estelle Barrett and Barbara Bolt (2010, 6) maintain that the "co-collaboration" that happens in making relies as much on matter and form as it does on the human dimensions of the process.

Making requires a knowledge of craft and material that develops over time through experience and improvisation with tools and materials (Carter 2004), an ability to put things together in creative, intuitive ways while relying as much on embodiment and emotions as on invention and skill—maybe even more so. Here I refer back to earlier chapters where practices like seeing things in a new light (chapter 2) or disrupting moments of dissensus (chapter 3) or hopeful imaginative practices (chapter 4) lead to making as a culmination of feelings and thoughts. What drives seeing, disrupting, and hoping are sensory and affective responses and intensities. Framing making in terms of these responses and intensities privileges thinking through making rather than the other way around—thinking as emerging through the act of improvising and feeling with materials. In making anything, from drawing a picture to writing prose to coding with Makey Makey,[1] it is the intensity, investment, and felt sensibilities of making that lead to ways of being and knowing.

MAKING AS TECHNÉ

The "maker movement" refers to a growing international trend in schools and community hubs such as libraries and malls, where children and adolescents share practices in the creative design and production of artifacts using physical and digital materials (Halverson and Sheridan 2014). The field of making and makerspaces has been gaining momentum over the past decade (Halverson and Sheridan 2014; Kafai, Fields, and Searle 2014; Peppler and Bender 2013). In this chapter, I build on this educator and researcher–led grassroots movement in an effort to embrace creative production and design through materials and technologies. Part of the drive for makerspace pedagogies rests on the realization that networked communicational systems and technologies demand new pedagogies. There is need both for alternative ways to plan, arrange, and orchestrate pedagogical time and space and for quite radical shifts in how content is framed and learned. Maker approaches to teaching and learning provide the freedom to play, experiment, tinker, and exchange ideas with peers over longer periods of time in both formal and informal spaces (Marsh et al. 2017).

Although makerspaces and maker approaches to teaching and learning are often associated with the traditions of cognitive psychology, constructivism, and experiential learning and linked to the writings of John Dewey (1902) and Seymour Papert (1980), in recent years, there has been significant empirical research on them (see Marsh et al. 2017). In this chapter, I try to expand definitions of making and maker approaches to take into greater account affect, posthumanism, and new materialism (Ehret 2018b), attending as well to growing efforts in the field of literacy studies to expand definitions of meaning making into post-structural and posthuman perspectives on the framings of making and design work. This is important because there has been an overemphasis in multiliteracies

1. Makey Makey invention kits each include a circuit board, alligator clips, and a USB cable to permit users to connect everyday objects such as bananas and bristol boards to computer programs.

scholarship on representation at the expense of nonrepresentation (Leander and Boldt 2013). I have therefore married maker movement work with affect in focusing more on senses and embodied maker work.

In theorizing "making" across this chapter's featured research studies, I draw on scholarship from the affect turn in literacy studies (Ehret 2018a; Leander and Boldt 2013; Lewis and Tierney 2013) to analyze processes of making as techné (Delagrange 2011; see glossary)—as a series of flows and intensities in which people orient inquiry around ontologies of becoming (Ehret 2018a, 2018b), as opposed to doing or knowing. Chapters 3 and 4 pushed for an understanding of literacy as felt and sensed with much less emphasis on knowledge development, and this chapter extends this framing of living literacies. Affect and embodiment play a role in this, as does allowing the space and time for serendipitous ideas and relational moments to unfold (Rowsell and Shillitoe 2019). The emphasis here is on a "What if ... ?" state of mind that grows and evolves as young people engage in maker work.

In using "techné" as a term for design work within my research, I place the focus on processes rather than on products. Susan H. Delagrange (2011) theorizes technologies as embedded within webs of social and cultural contexts, where they have agency and intra-act (Barad 2007) with people in active, entangled, sensed, and lived ways. Techné permits these moments of intellectual work to meet with practical work—when knowledge in heads intersects with craft through hands and bodies. Techné allows for embodied relationships across people, places, events, and material artifacts that are in play as people make meaning. There is a dynamic quality to these moments of inquiry which draw on senses and tacit modalities. William Covino (1988) calls them "the art of wondering" and Delagrange (2011, 13), "an epistemic technology of wonder." Acts of wonder emerge from open, unstructured time with technologies and materials to imagine "What if ... ?" (see chapter 4) kinds of designs within makerspaces.

The art of wondering stems from techné work. Indeed, techné *is* wonder: an attitude toward the world that predisposes us to amazement and to learn its causes. Wonder is primarily a visual practice, and, through it, I pursue an embodied techné. In other words, wonder invites associative thinking that ushers in feelings, beliefs, tinkering, materialities, and nonmaterialities with a fluidity driven by heart and head work (Shillitoe

2018). Emotions, arrangements, bodies, and, most of all, visuals swirl about during techné; they flow into the art of wondering, where they get registered on the body (Massumi 2015).

RESEARCH STUDIES WITHIN MAKER LITERACIES

Of the three research studies featured in this chapter, the first, "Maker Literacies," has been conducted in multiple cities in the Niagara region, including St. Catharines, Welland, and Thorold, since 2017 and is planned to run through 2021 (see "Chapter 7 Featured Studies" in appendix). The study involves five different projects, each with a focus on a specific mode, conducted with professionals in the creative and media sectors who coplanned and cotaught units of study and projects with teachers that students completed over four to six weeks. Modes represented in "Maker Literacies" are documentary filmmaking (with a documentary filmmaker, a psychotherapist, and a grade 11 English teacher); graphic story and animated film (with a graphic story writer, an animated film producer, and a grade 3/4 teacher); coding (with a professional coder and a grade five teacher); videogame design (with videogame designers and two ninth grade teachers); and conceptual portraiture and interpretive photography (with a photographer and a grade 11/12 visual arts teacher and his students). Each project involves a maker approach to learning and teaching with materials and technologies provided and ample time for play, creativity, problem solving, and peer interactions. In addition, a key dimension of the research involves scaffolding (see glossary) and modeling by professionals and teachers (and the research team) with students as they gradually design texts in a particular project's mode (e.g., a documentary film). Amélie Lemieux and I are the lead researchers. Together, we have taken detailed ethnographic field notes, conducted interviews, and analyzed a large corpus of student-made multimodal compositions. The chapter's second featured study, drawn on to illustrate making, is "Resettled Literacies," which took place in the winter of 2018 and involved fifteen refugees who completed a series of multimodal compositions in a welcome center in St. Catharines (see appendix). Julianne Burgess and I conducted the research. Once a week Julianne focused on a multimodal activity, such as conceptual photography, and I assisted with the teaching and took ethnographic field notes. Vignettes from these different research studies are interspersed throughout to illustrate our research teams' theorizing of making. Each vignette features aspects of making as a lived practice.

LIONEL AND HIS FLIPBOOK

As part of the "Maker Literacies" research study, Amélie Lemieux, Larry Swartz (graphic story writer and scholar), Melissa Turcotte (grade 3/4 teacher), Jennifer Burkitt (media production and animated film producer), and I conducted a six-week project in the autumn of 2017 entitled "Speech Bubbles, Graphic Stories, Flipbooks, Storyboards" (see table 7.1). Working with a graphic story writer and an animated film producer, grade 3/4 students completed a succession of assignments that moved from classic comic techniques such as knock-knock jokes all the way to short animated films produced in Pixton (comic software) and Toontastic (animated film app). Over six weeks, students in the third grade class learned about graphic and animated filmic features such as speech bubbles, close-ups, thought bubbles, sound effects, and medium shots as they worked in pairs and groups of three, taking on standard roles in the animation industry as outlined by Jennifer (e.g., Foley artist, sound engineer, copywriter, animated and visual effects editors). The research was framed by the following research questions: What happens when students move from a graphic story to an animated film? What happens during transmodal moments when a student moves from one mode into another mode? What is gained and what is lost when shifting across modes?

Working together with Melissa for two years, these grade 3/4 students knew one another well, and this familiarity played out strongly in the research. I found a group of boys who were best friends one moment and fought the next to be particularly interesting; one of them who stood out was Lionel (as with other chapters, participant pseudonyms are used throughout this chapter as well). Lionel has an avid imagination and often told something along the lines of what Alexandra Georgakopoulou (2007, 190) calls "small stories":

> ... stories that have not made it to the mainstream of narrative and identity analysis, yet they abound as well as being crucial sites of subjectivity in everyday

Table 7.1. Outline of speech bubbles, graphic stories, flipbooks, storyboards

Literacy event	Materials/mentor(s)	Practices
Create knock-knock joke books	• Larry Swartz • Knock-knock jokes (distributed independently) • Paper and markers	• Students read and choose a knock-knock joke • Minibooklets created from 8½" x 11" sheets (folded to create five pages) • Knock-knock jokes, two presented with speech bubbles and two with characters
Community read	• *SOS! Titanic!* by Frieda Wishinsky	• Teacher's read aloud novel
Four-panel graphic page	• Excerpted pages of novel *SOS! Titanic!* distributed to each student on 8½" x 11" paper with markers	• Paper folded twice to create four panels • Students transformed novel text into graphic pages featuring speech bubbles
Close-up look at graphic texts	• Short graphic novel distributed to each student • Worksheet graphic treasure hunt	• Teacher demonstrates text features • In pairs, students investigate text features of graphic texts by completing worksheet
Reading group	• Five titles from Canadian Flyer Adventures series	• Students arranged in groups of four or five • Guided reading and literature circle
Author visit	• Author Frieda Wishinsky	• Interview with author (whole class) • One-to-one sharing with author and students
Create graphic pages using templates	• Template of graphic pages (four or six panels) • Excerpts from novel read as a group	• Students independently create graphic pages of novel excerpts
Moving into digital domain—Pixton	• Jennifer Burkitt and her helpers • Chrome books • Pixton	• Work with Pixton app • Create avatars and dialogue

Literacy event	Materials/mentor(s)	Practices
Make flipbooks	• Sticky notes • Colored pencils and markers	• Watch YouTube on making flipbooks • Make flipbooks and share with group
Storyboards	• Large sheets of paper • Markers	• Talk about adapting *Arctic Storm* chapter to a storyboard • Draw out setup, conflict, challenge, climax, and resolution
Animated text—Toontastic storytelling app	• Chrome books with Toontastic	• Work in small groups and create animated texts and share with adults and classmates

Source: Rowsell et al. 2018, table 1.

interactional contexts. By labelling those stories as "small," there is a distinctiveness, both interactionally and as an antidote to the tradition of "grand" narratives research.

Lionel and his friends could frequently be heard exchanging small stories, which were crucial for two reasons: first, they took on a life of their own and were often driven by affect and emotions in the midst of making something; and, second, they relied on agency, performing, and positioning agency in the classroom. Speaking to the affective dimension, emotions sparked one boy to tell a story that sparked another to tell another story in a trail of stories that almost certainly were not entirely true and that, at the very least, contained embellishments. Lionel was particularly prone to concocting elaborate stories, and I loved hearing them and especially how animated he became in telling them. Speaking to agentive dimensions, small stories were important because they gave us a window into students' thinking, their abundant creativity, and their intuitive understandings about making. One such example occurred when Lionel told me about his flipbook story (see figure 7.1).

There were three boys who built a campfire, the story goes, and they put marshmallows on sticks to toast them over it. But, as one boy leans down to push his marshmallow farther in, his hair catches fire. The boy yells for help, but, instead of extinguishing the fire on his head, the other

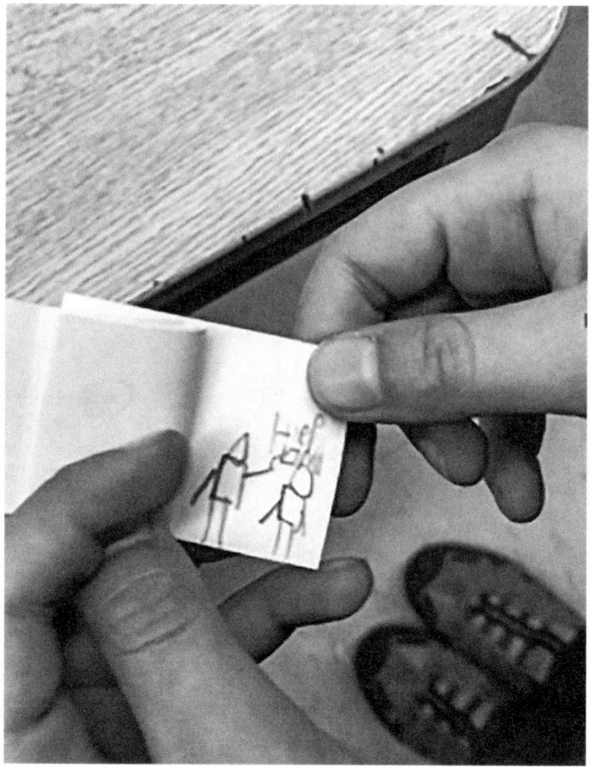

Figure 7.1
Lionel makes his flipbook

boys use it to further toast their marshmallows. When Lionel recounted the story to me, we both laughed and talked about how original it was and how challenging it was to construct the story on twenty-four tiny Post-it pages, with small, subtle changes on each little page.

Within his small story, there is techné in the moment, with Lionel's making through inquiry; there is a story arc (i.e., intro, denouement, and finale); and there is craft knowledge on display, linked to Lionel's lived literacy practices away from school. Lionel's pictures of the boys by the campfire were detailed enough to show their facial expressions, with even traces of Edvard Munch's *The Scream* on some of the tiny pages. I discovered that Lionel made similar small stories on larger sheets of paper at home and that he enjoyed creating and designing them as a part of his everyday. This practice reminded me of a research study years before in a Toronto school when I met Ahmed and his mum, Rihana, and they talked about Ahmed's creation of flyers at home (Rowsell and Pahl 2007), which led to a theory of "sedimented identities" that Kate and I developed in our work.

The lesson to be drawn from Lionel's small story on his Post-it note multimodal flipbook is that this specific design would not have been possible without the combined forces of friends encouraging him, Jennifer Burkitt's lesson on Post-it note flipbook designs, the material affordances of little pages turning to make a story, and Lionel's passion, affect, and thoughts in the process. The example throws into relief elements that inform making and living literacies: everyday stories; relational moments; some degree of craft knowledge and techné; affect and emotion; and acts of wonderment.

Materials put together and made into something are a realization of people, stuff, and practices. Form and materials meld into each other. Bodies, built forms, and social meanings are active properties within compositions. Having examined similar moments when compositions were made and unmade, Christian Ehret, Ty Hollett, and Robin Jocius (2016, 371) speak of "the unpredictable intra-actions of moving bodies–materials, including chairs, fans, and dirt." There is a constant ebb and flow of animate and inanimate forces at work when making.

THE STORY BEHIND THE HELMET AND THE SCARF

Julianne Burgess and Jennifer Rowsell

Moving to a second featured research study, "Resettled Literacies," with fifteen refugees taking language lessons at a welcome center in St. Catharines, Julianne and I conducted the research from January until April 2018 (see appendix) to explore multimodal approaches to language development with a group of adult newcomer English language learners. Over the course of the study, emotional and affective intensities emerged in response to a range of issues such as the stark contrasts between the participants' former lives in their homelands and their new lives in Canada. For our first session, Julianne created a gallery walk in the welcome center space with pictures all around the room from an exhibition she had attended in Ottawa. The exhibit featured the works of Gohar Dashti, an Iranian photographer who takes provocative photos of her life in Iran, such as a man and woman having a picnic on a minefield or a Muslim woman carrying a boom box. Given that most of our participants came from Iran, Iraq, and Syria, we felt that the Dashti photos would speak to them and arouse their interest. After looking at them, the participants broke into smaller groups to discuss specific images in the photos and what they meant or suggested to them. We held a general group discussion to speculate on what was taking place in each photo and how the individuals in each felt, as a form of group reflection, after which the smaller groups then re-created their own versions of the photos.

The participants in this group chose to include two of their members—Yana and Adara—in the group's re-created photo and found materials to clothe them, extending the story of the original photo to be about a couple reuniting after war, as seen in figure 7.2. The original photo in the museum has a long silk scarf hanging on a hook and a helmet beside it on another hook. There are no people in the original photograph.

Quietly and methodically, Yana and Adara staged the couple's reunion after the war, facing each other, wearing props that represented the

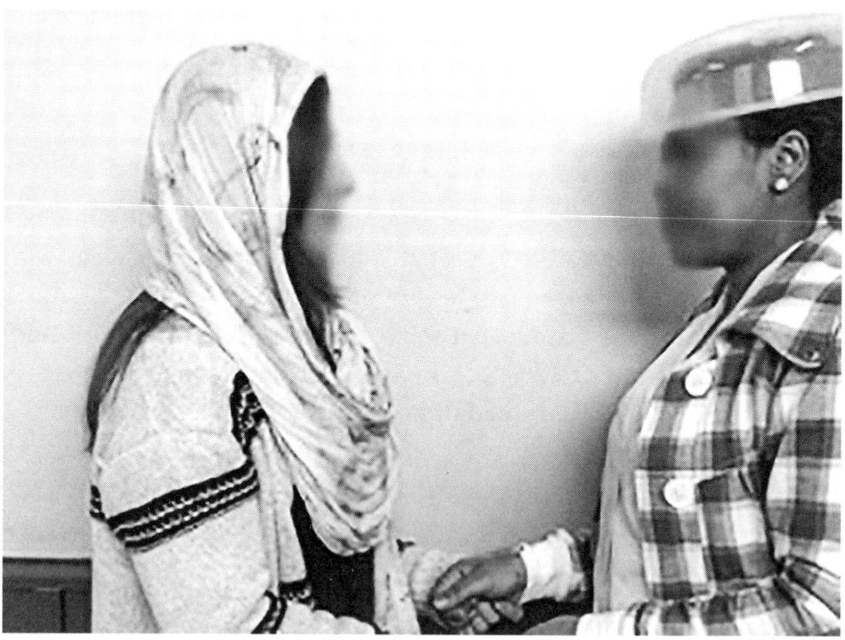

Figure 7.2
Returning from war

original scarf and helmet. Although they are not smiling in the photo, Yana and Adara insisted that the couple was happy, but that it was a bittersweet reunion. "They are a family and there was a war, and the father had to leave the family to go to war," Yana explained. "He returns to his family. The wife says: 'Why did you leave me?' She wears the scarf that he took with him to war." The essential message of the photo relied on people, objects, and visual techniques, but what interested us is how careful Yana and Adara were in choosing artifacts, deportment, facial expressions, gestures, and the ways that they crafted their small stories.

Julianne and I regarded this session with newcomer Canadians as possessing the ingredients of making and maker work in that there was some instruction as well as modeling and scaffolding; there were materials at hand to make; there was freedom and space to tinker, think, and produce a multimodal image; and stories became etched in the image. Digging deeper, what pushed the making for participants were the visceral feelings that each group experienced as they planned and produced their photos based on Dashti's photographs.

* * *

DECONSTRUCTING THE MAKER MOVEMENT

As referred to earlier, maker movement philosophy and pedagogy draw on Nordic models of learning through do-it-yourself (DIY) and problem solving—often in studio spaces. Jackie Marsh ran the European Commission–funded "MakEY" project in sixteen countries around the world that enacted maker work and examined young children's digital literacy and creative skills through their participation in creative activities in specially designed spaces called "makerspaces" (Marsh et al. 2017).

There are diverse approaches within the maker movement, from treating making as rooted in tinkering, problem solving, inventing, and fostering entrepreneurship to treating it as more rooted within culture and identity (Anderson 2012). The former approach focuses on making's products; the latter, on its practices and ways of knowing. Within maker movement literature, the key essential ideas are often expressed using verbs such as "make," "share," "tinker," and "play." Makerspace research has tended to be conflated with technology, innovation, and entrepreneurism, casting makerspaces as transforming the world of learning. Although such a product-oriented approach is positive, my living literacies colleagues and I prefer a more culturally infused approach to making to locate it within contexts and people's lives. There are maker movement researchers, such as Yasmin Kafai, Deborah Fields, and Kristin Searle (2014) and Erica Rosenfeld Halverson and Kimberley M. Sheridan (2014), who have shown that making and maker movement approaches can challenge what counts as legitimate learning. For example, Kafai, Fields, and Searle (2014) talk about e-textiles as "disruptive" making activities that bring both "hard" and "soft" skills to the maker ecology, expanding our understanding of what counts as making.

To enact a maker approach to learning and experiencing makerspaces, my colleagues at Brock University and I (Figg et al. 2018) planned and staged three makerspace days in the spring of 2017 (see "Makerspace Research Days" under "Chapter 7 Featured Studies" in appendix). There were three makerspace events: one with preservice teachers (teachers in training) and faculty; another with grade 3 students and their teachers; and a third one with preservice teachers and faculty open to the public. The small research study gave me a window into the makerspace world and the kinds of practices, processes, and ways of knowing that people apply to makerspace thinking. The research involved documenting practices and epistemologies in field notes and interviews with individuals who attended the events. Figure 7.3 features images from the makerspace days. Inside the large gymnasium housing the three events, there was a wide variety of makerspace stations involving: a Dash and Dot robot; 3-D printing; immersive world or wearable devices; textiles and sewing; duct tape; beadwork; woodwork; Makey Makey activities; green screening; and coding. Attendees spent thirty minutes at each station and then moved on to a new one. The research team circulated around the stations, conducting interviews and taking field notes.

Although attendees enjoyed the open, do-it-yourself nature of each makerspace station, the activities felt mindful and calming to them, rather than actively arousing their thinking. As noted previously, there are different types of makerspaces in libraries, public spaces, and classrooms, and there are pop-up makerspaces in any environment. A popular rendering of makerspaces in policy is based on constructivism, design thinking,

Figure 7.3
Top: Robot station (left), greenscreen station (right); bottom: arts and crafts station (left), weaving station (right)

collaborative learning, and media literacy, relying heavily on epistemic tropes such as problem solving, learning by doing, studio time, and digital and nondigital worlds (Papert 1993), which are certainly valuable and key components of making.

Nonetheless, a number of makerspace attendees shared that, for them, the inherent appeal of makerspace activities lay in the social or relational nature of making things with arts and crafts materials as well as technologies. There was a "quilting bee" feel (as one interviewee put it) to these activities, where people felt both at ease to chit-chat about politics and backgrounds and connected to such things as colors and swatches of fabric (I noted each of these observations while at makerspace stations). Many of the conversations I overheard dealt with combining materials in novel ways. As one attendee expressed it, the makerspace activities were "open ended, but conversations pull you in and make you reflect on the inception of a design, designs, how designs make you feel and how they map onto interests … so you kind of solve things through the social" (Suzanne, March 25, 2017). There appeared to be a natural rhythm to activities at makerspace activity stations, and at the heart of it was a circulation between attention, motion, and action and between thinking, attention, emotion, and action. Part of this rhythm involved risks, failures and uncertainties that were tolerable, even welcome.

Another makerspace attendee viewed her experience differently: "I liked the design process because I am familiar with analog and old ways of doing things, but with makerspaces, there is a little bit more of fear, of taking risks and therefore investing yourself in the process" (Megan, March 25, 2017). Suzanne (March 25, 2017) maintained that, for her, taking on "digital making" felt like learning a second language, whereas the young children in her classroom "are brought up with both physical and digital languages." As a teacher, Suzanne emphasizes flexibility with her students because she shapes her program around student interests and she believes that these interests increasingly deal with digital worlds and communicational practices.

MATERIALIZING PRACTICES

Thinking back to the grade 3 student Lionel who made flipbooks and to how he became interested and invested and exhibited ways of knowing and being through making when he developed a story, it was in observing and talking about Lionel's materializing practices that I got to know him and to recognize his way into inquiry and techné. Through humor, small drawings, interactions with his friends, laughter, and flipping the small Post-it pages rapidly with his fingers, Lionel materialized a multimodal composition.

When artists and media professionals team up with educators to frame materials, what often results is a combination of explicit and tacit knowledge (Rowsell 2013). Estelle Barrett and Barbara Bolt (2010, 5) talk about materializing practices as an "ongoing performative engagement and productivity both at moments of production and consumption." Materializing practices reveals knowledge in the making as individuals work with materials, embedding in them their own subjectivities, belief systems, and sense-laden responses. Knowledge is generated through action and reflection, which often mark the start of meaning making (Barrett and Bolt 3020, 5). Problem, context, and solution are all braided together during this process. Paul Carter (2004) talks about material thinking as handling materials in practice; Tim Ingold (2007, 2008), about a material productivity that can be catalyzed by sensory engagement with materials and modes in the moment. To illustrate material productivity, I offer a vignette from the "Maker Literacies" study.

BEN MAKES HIS SCRATCH/MAKEY MAKEY STORY

In the winter of 2018, Amélie Lemieux, Joel Gritter, Ann Rigg, and I completed a coding project over six weeks at an elementary school in the Niagara region. The project began with children reading short stories, followed by their watching stories coded in Scratch[2] and then writing stories of their own. A technology consultant for the District School Board of Niagara, Ann, taught the students how to code in Scratch, after which they coded the stories they had written. Finally, using Makey Makey kits, the students added animations to their stories.

From the beginning of the coding project eleven-year-old Ben, who had immigrated to Canada from China, was engrossed in making his

2. Developed by researchers at MIT, Scratch software allows users to produce their own interactive stories and animations.

story. As an English language learner, Ben struggled to keep up with his classmates, but, using Scratch and being a big fan of basketball, he was able to write and code a simple short story about Kyrie Irving, Lebron James, James Harden, and Stephen Curry shooting hoops. Figure 7.4 shows Ben working with Ann on his Makey Makey poster, which he had coded in Scratch. Composing the story gave Ben a chance to engage with his passion for basketball and embed outside interests into his schoolwork. He gravitated more to the digital than the material work, such as cutting out photos, gluing them on bristol board (folder stock), and writing out names. Ben enjoyed figuring out codes through trial and error, problem solving in Scratch, and making action figures (basketball players) move around on-screen. There was a dynamic materiality (Walsh and Simpson 2013) to the work he completed, and he learned through clicking or touch (Crescenzi, Jewitt, and Price 2014; Wohlwend 2015) how to figure out codes and embed visuals. His knowing through making emerged from the coding he completed and his material work on the

Figure 7.4
Ben and Ann working on Ben's coding project

bristol board. Most importantly, however, Ben felt at ease, confident, and adept moving across the story writing, coding, and arts and crafts work—something he had not felt when he engaged in more traditional writing activities at his school.

ORDINARY AFFECT

What draws someone into sense making? What is the difference between just getting something done and actually investing in the process of composing, designing and making—and getting lost in it? A strong element of that difference has to do with what Kathleen Stewart (2007) describes as "ordinary affect." Offering insights into aspects of everyday affect that are as unpredictable as they are intense and textured, Stewart builds "idiosyncratic maps" of the connections between singularities in affect that people experience across time and space. She maintains that "affect is not so much forms of signification, or units of knowledge, as … expressions of ideas or problems performed as a kind of involuntary and powerful learning and participation" (Stewart (2007, 40).

Ordinary affect gives "circuits and flows the forms of a life" (Stewart 2007, 2); it invites your past memories to bubble up while you are engaged in practices, and these memories can shift your mood—or not. "The ordinary can happen before the mind can think" (Stewart 2007, 5). As something that can be imagined as much as inhabited, ordinary affect ushers in knowing, making, and being in powerful ways. There are always stories to tell, create, and live through. *Living Literacies* shares many such stories as illustrations of lived literacies. What I find particularly generative about ordinary affect as Stewart conceives it is its tacitness, its mercurial uncertainness, and, most of all, its capacity for evolving and becoming. For me, making relies heavily on ordinary affect insofar as the living of everyday life moment by moment invites in past memories and present felt sensibilities—and makes future imaginings possible. The next few sections draw on research that throws ordinary affect into relief.

THIS DOCUMENTARY ACTUALLY MAKES WELLAND LOOK GOOD

In the autumn of 2017, Amélie Lemieux, Tara Markovich (a secondary school teacher), Vanessa Crosbie-Ramsay (a documentary filmmaker), and I coproduced a documentary film with grade 11 students at a high school in Welland, Ontario, as part of the "Maker Literacies" research study. Welland is often disparaged for its high unemployment and serious addiction and mental health issues. Rather than dwell on its deficits, however, our research team wanted instead to celebrate the city's strengths. To do this, Tara and I decided to start the project by having our students read the Canadian young adult novel *Shattered* by Eric Walters, which depicts the friendship between a homeless war veteran and a teenager from an affluent family who learns about what it means to struggle with mental health issues, poverty, and displacement. When they had finished reading the novel, a psychotherapist came into their classroom to talk about what happens when someone suffers from PTSD and severe anxiety, after which the fifteen students were introduced to documentary filmmaking by Vanessa. Four groups then produced documentary films based on both the novel and what they had learned about addiction and mental health issues. The students were so pleased with the final *Maker Literacies* documentary we coproduced together that Beyoncé (her choice of pseudonym) declared: "This documentary actually makes Welland look good."

In exploring techné, acts of wonderment, and ordinary affect, the research study provided a close-up of choices the students made as they produced their three-minute documentaries on one of the study's key themes. Bella, who has anxiety herself, which made it difficult for her to concentrate at school and get things done, knew from the outset what she wanted to focus on for her documentary. She worked with two other young women, Ruby and Gill, and, despite disagreements between Bella and Ruby, the three of them were clear about how they wanted to film their short documentary and how they would use materials and spaces to produce it. They knew they were going to focus on eating disorders and body image. They knew they would incorporate some improvisation in two scenes: one featured a teacher and student talking about anxiety, and the other took place in the school gym. Finally, they knew their documentary would be factual. Using a green screen, iPads, props, and different outfits, the three young women filmed footage, chose still photos, and produced voiceovers. Techné came into play when they filmed different versions of their performances and discussed which one worked best across the film's narrative. Tensions arose when Ruby, a big fan of his work, insisted on incorporating images of Cory Monteith. A cast member in the TV show *Glee*, Monteith died of an overdose in 2013, and Ruby wanted to embed a small tribute to him in the documentary. But Bella felt such a tribute was too unrelated to their main topic. A compromise was brokered to pipe in some of a Monteith song that related to anxiety and to briefly include his image. Another moment of ordinary affect happened when I followed the group to the school gym, where their filming while other students were working out created some awkwardness. These small, human moments during making surfaced varying flows of feelings, and some, such as the (much shortened) tribute to Montieth, were materialized in the produced text. There were many similar small but meaningful examples of techné and acts of wonderment that happened during filming the documentaries when different students in the class shared how documentary filmmaking made them see their hometown in a new light, and how what they took away from the project and from working with professionals was powerful.

MAKING, KNOWING, BECOMING THROUGH LIVING LITERACIES

To teach based on living literacies, educators could offer students longer blocks of time to design and make multimodal texts, allowing for a "what if state of mind" (referred to earlier in chapter 4 on hoping). *What if* I take this sheet of cardboard and use it to make a hydraulic arm? *What if* I use these rubber bands to make a propeller car? Or *what if* I code a basketball player's movements across the court and then mirror these movements through cut-and-pasted bristol board forms? Everyday materials combine the comfort of familiar things (Miller 2008) with the playfulness of do-it-yourself tinkering that can lead to acts of wonderment. Distilled down, making entails these kinds of fluid, continuous, passion-driven practices that mix reason with sensation. Though design work clearly involves materializing a thought or idea, since emotions often define what people choose to see and not to see, a driving force of design work is making through sensual and affective engagement.

Things made, in whatever mode, express values, backgrounds, and beliefs. As people make, there is a dance between thinking and feeling through space and time and between knowing and not knowing and through just trying things out. Making is therefore less about the stuff or materials or tools of makerspaces and more about thinking and feeling through modalities. Elizabeth Ellsworth (2005, 30) talks about making as "processual paths" to be walked, or as interrogative designs that modulate in intensity. Thus there is a push and pull of inside and outside worlds whenever someone is involved in the process of making or designing.

Working closely with Vanessa Crosbie Ramsay (the documentary filmmaker referred to earlier), I found that many of her conversations with project students involved how to capture emotions, moods, feelings within shots. In Vanessa's words (December 2017): "I think as an artist if there's no emotion or anything behind it then you can make something that's very technically proficient, but does not have a heart or soul then have you accomplished something worthwhile?"

But how do compositions acquire a heart and a soul? Is it through the materials, modes, or physical features that a composer brings together? Is it the affective intensities and flows that culminate into a composition? Or do heart and soul derive from a composer's moments of inspiration that lead to a finished work? In so much making work, the social plays an essential role in terms of affect, whether this involves students working together or professionals and teachers planning activities and lessons or teachers and professionals working with students. These are the relational moments that stick and that imprint lasting impressions. Christian Ehret (2018a) maintains that affect serves as a social force during these moments of becoming and wonderment, and Sara Ahmed (2014) sees social relations as the glue of making. But time plays a fundamental role, too: "If literacy through the event is known through the feeling of a potential for relational transformation, then this feeling includes the feeling of time[, although] time feels different than its constructed, linear representations" (Ehret 2018a, 15).

It is through affect, however, that Ehret (2018a, 2018b) provides literacy studies with a way of theorizing the ubiquitous notion of the "literacy event" (Heath 1983). Framing literacy events through flows and intensities of affect imbues "the idiosyncratic, irrational affects that give events the very feeling of mattering, and that generate and sustain the human desiring that makes reading, writing, and social change *feel* essential" (Ehret 2018a, 8). Time plays a role in such theorizing, harkening back to Jay Lemke's work (2000) on the shorter and longer timescales of objects, with the longer timescales carrying more memories, significance, and felt sensibilities.

Making often starts with an idea driven by an outside force like a teacher or professional (as in the "Maker Literacies" vignettes) or an inside force like an interest or a familiar practice. Once making starts, it catalyzes techné (Delagrange 2011) as a process of inquiry that invites small stories, which serve as substantive or conceptual anchors for the making. Deciding on a small story frequently invites relational or connective moments and conversations. It is during and before these interactions that some emotional intensities get stuck (Ahmed 2014) and entangled into the making and strongly inform what gets made. But emotions do not always stick within relations and interactions; they can also be subjectively driven between people and materials. The next research vignette illustrates the notion of affectively driven literacy events as well as shorter and longer timescales.

ADARA AND HER PRAYER BEADS

Thinking back to the "Resettled Literacies" study with refugees described earlier, one session was devoted to an activity called "Every object tells a story" (Pahl and Rowsell 2010). One of the study participants, Adara, shared an artifact that she values and that tells a story from her past—prayer beads, which she carries with her everywhere she goes. She spoke about their igniting flows of experiences and memories that emerged at unpredictable times, sometimes when she was in the midst of meaning making and at other times when she was not. Moreover, the prayer beads represented a longer timescale for her, dating back to when she was still at home in Syria. Lemke (2000) talks about how individuals have shorter and longer timescales with material objects. Shorter timescales are moments of meaning making that are less significant and whose histories and connections are limited compared with longer timescales, which are memory and sense laden. Lemke (2000) offers the example of a regular kitchen knife (shorter timescale) juxtaposed with a samurai sword (longer timescale) as telling examples of material objects that carry shorter and longer timescales, respectively.

Returning to Adara, a family friend gave her the prayer beads when Adara's son was very ill eight years earlier, and she always had them with her as a constant reminder about a challenging period before she left Syria to resettle in the Niagara region. There is an energy and vitality to the prayer beads (see figure 7.5) that would not be present with an object that Adara had encountered in a passing moment at school or during a fleeting exchange on the street.

The prayer beads carried with them strong affect; the digital story Adara crafted after our session together let her visually materialize her thoughts, feelings, and embodied reactions with respect to them.

To conclude this chapter, I encourage a lived perspective on making that invites resilience and criticality, drawing on the work of Kris Gutiérrez (2016, 187), who talks about an urgent need today "for new

Figure 7.5
Adara's prayer beads have a long history

systems that demand radical shifts in our views of learning and in our perceptions of youth from non-dominant communities so that they can become agents of newly imagined futures." Resilience in this instance means both reflecting on the present by accounting for qualitative differences between now and yesterday and also revisiting and reassessing policies and pedagogies that no longer meet our needs. Gutiérrez (2016, 187) insists that designing educational possibilities for social change entails designs that "squarely address issues of cultural diversity, social inequality, and robust learning." To that end, researchers need to examine social contexts and meaning-making processes, to focus their efforts on informing and improving "the human condition of which learning is fundamental," and to develop repertoires of literacy that speak to what Gutiérrez calls a "sociocultural imagination"—in short, they need to have an expansive understanding of how people learn (Gutiérrez 2016, 188). Such an understanding pushes for "creating and sustaining learning environments where mind in action is privileged rather than mind as simply bounded in the individual" (Gutiérrez 2016, 188). Thinking about making and about resilience relies heavily on diversity as capital to be leveraged and exploited. Or, as Gutiérrez (2016, 192) tells us: "Social transformation shifts from the focus on 'fixing' people and their communities to a focus on the reorganization of systems of activity in which participants can become designers."

CONCLUSION: APPLYING A LIVING LITERACIES APPROACH

Jennifer Rowsell and Kate Pahl

Research, then, has a task to do in making visible the complexity of local, everyday, community literacy practices and challenging dominant stereotypes and myopia.

—Brian Street (2010, 22)

In *Living Literacies*, we have located our thinking strongly in the sites and spaces of our research. We have also focused more on research processes and less on theory. Our aim has been to produce both a "how to" book—how to live literacy research—and a book that sets out a theory of literacy based on everyday life. Our work has therefore been situated in our own practice. In trying to characterize a living literacies approach, we have drawn on research studies we have conducted over the past decade or so; our approach has developed over the course of these studies and coalesced at specific moments during them, and it relies heavily on a sense of place.

Our key epiphany is that sites and spaces—places—can generate theory about literacy. Layered with histories and memories, places can draw out affect and call up ideas, memories, narratives, and imagined futures (Massey 2005). Rotherham and St. Catharines have been the places we have focused on. Although one of the places is in the United Kingdom and the other in Canada, they have similar profiles in that, associated with stories of trauma and tragedy featured in the press, both have been portrayed in a negative light and regarded as marginal when compared to larger, neighboring places. At the same time, Rotherham and St. Catharines are filled with promise, hope, and care, and their residents are often eager to defend the histories of their hometowns and tell alternative stories about them. These two places have been gifts for us as researchers because we have been able to work with their children, teenagers, and adults who have wanted to see them in a new, reimagined light (Campbell et al. 2018). This has been fundamental to our efforts to frame living literacies.

In the preceding chapters, we have situated people as embodied identities who see, feel, hope, create, make, and know within diverse landscapes and whose realities and lived experiences differ vastly. As Jennifer and Terry noted in "Seeing" (chapter 2), the ways in which people's experiences and place-based knowledge materialize in photographs signal key aspects of how they live literacy. Sarah Pink often depicts ethnographic research as a slow journey into "the materiality and sociality of the research encounter" (Pink 2006, 34). In *Living Literacies*, we have attended to the sociality and sensoriality of place first and to its materialities after, and we have prioritized this perspective over others to analyze the *lived* nature of literacies. Many of the examples we have presented—the "adventure playground," experiences of the street, the maker days—are located in communities, and an understanding of the specificities of context and lived experiences is entwined in our research. Thus our own affective experiences mesh with our accounts of literacy. In Kate's dialogue with Zanib (chapter 3), the concept of the literacies of activism emerges as a multifaceted and complex set of ideas that rest on divergent histories and experiences.

Underlying our living literacies approach to research and practice are a belief in the situated, embodied, and ideological, as opposed to autonomous, models of literacy (Street 1995) and an abiding hope that literacy, as a verb, will come alive through people and their habits, experiences, and ways of being and knowing. This hope connects strongly with Brian Street's utopian conception of literacy as always to come (Street 1997). In "Hoping" (chapter 4), we see literacy as something that can be grasped through practice necessarily placed in the "not yet" (Bloch [1918] 1986). As Street (1997, 56) aptly observes: "We are not just neutral observers, but social beings already inscribed with culturally influenced manifestations of the deeper fears and desires that influence all human life." He shows how literacy practices are patterned and persistent as much as they are diverse and vernacular, and that an emphasis on *real* literacies as they are *lived,* as opposed to artificial or formal forms of universal literacy, locates literacy as a social practice.

It is one thing to theorize lived literacies and even to illustrate them within research, but it is quite another to apply a living literacies approach, as we have, across learning sites such as schools. Teaching through such an approach makes literacy come alive. It enables students at any age to see, disrupt, create, know, hope, and make in ways that support their own agency and how they mediate the agency of others. Literacy is both a noun and a verb, echoing Street's insight that culture, too, is a verb (Street 1993b). Seeing cultures and literacies as entwined has helped us expand definitions of what literacy could be. Our work together has encouraged us to think of literacy as seeing, disrupting, hoping, knowing, creating, and making—a multifaceted concept that transforms as practice changes across sites and spaces.

A CALL TO ACTION FOR LITERACY EDUCATION

In an era when children as young as five are called out for not speaking in complete sentences, and "school readiness" is a watchword for a negative view of children's literacy capacities, we urgently need new ways of recognizing what literacy is, and how it can be harnessed to meet the demands of everyday life. Part of that challenge, however, is to ask ourselves: How do we want to live in the world? To deal with the challenges of rapid climate change, persistent inequality, and the failure of corporations and governments to respond to citizens' concerns, activism is needed. Young people live in a world not of their making with immense challenges ahead of them. The literacies of activism need to be not only recognized, but also honed to address these challenges. This requires new ways of knowing and making that make it possible for young people to reposition their learning and understanding, and central to these new ways is an expansive and nuanced understanding of what literacy could become.

Where we live creates a vocabulary for action and for pedagogy. Places like Rotherham and St. Catharines have a lot to teach us—if we could only listen. Part of this listening entails less obvious, more ephemeral aspects of life such as embodiment and affect. And part of this listening also entails respect for, and attention to, the nonhuman physical, natural, and material worlds. Our work has expanded to include the nonrepresentational aspects of literacy, where literacy is part of something wider—the arc of a gaze on a pair of feet, the swoop of a slide, or the silent stillness of a fishing rod. Within these spaces, however, literacy can grow. We have watched moments in our research when children and young people have harnessed often homegrown and small-scale ideas and expanded them through the processes of refining, making, and crafting, which in turn involve a literacy that expands and develops as well.

What we cannot do is turn our backs on how literacy is lived. This means engaging in research that is "with" rather than "on" participants, and we have enacted this in the coauthoring of this book. Our thinking also needs to engage not with literacy's set forms of script and notation, but with what literacy could be, with the hopeful literacies that involve "literacy desiring" (Kuby, Gutshall Rucker, and Kirchhofer 2015). This requires educators and literacy policy makers to become attuned to a conceptual framing of literacy as *lived*. Our hope is that, if they do, the emergent, messy stuff of literacy will become part of the experienced moment-by-moment unfolding of the literacy event. We have articulated theoretical tools that account for the "in the moment," the material, the nonrepresentational, and the speculative (Ehret 2018a; MacLure 2011; Truman 2019). These tools derive from perspectives honed through expanding our empirical gaze to include the nonhuman, the material, and the embodied. Our vision is for a version of literacy that is *in practice*—both lived and imagined.

LITERACIES IN PROCESS

As practice shifts, so does literacy, and so must we attune our understanding as researchers. We have argued that both research practices and theoretical tools must change and adapt to meet the world's greater challenges so that literacy, as lived, can evolve and become new all over again. We need to listen to the ephemeral, messy, and incomplete (Pahl 2002) and to the "roar that lies on the other side of silence" (Eliot [1871] 1965, 226). The tools we use to understand literacy in all its complexity are inadequate to the task of grasping literacies as they are formed and re-formed in the everyday. Our focus on the collaborative nature of literacy inquiry makes visible the need to account for who the definers of literacy are, and how literacy gets defined. These ways of knowing need to account for those who have less access to institutional definition (Nagar 2014). An expanded view of literacy can bring in multilingualism, gesture, materiality, oral stories, and intangible, felt affects (Enriquez et al. 2016). We advocate working at the edges of literacy, feeling our way, and walking with our coparticipants and co-researchers as a mode of inquiry. Advocating for lived experience and for ontological categories formed with participants in research projects might mean acknowledging complex linguistic heritages that are unwritten or undocumented. One of the reasons we need to do research with people in communities is that the books about the practices we find there have not yet been written. Literacy research is a utopian enterprise, one that finds its way in the half-glimpsed spaces of the "not yet." We need to listen to the ephemeral, the diverse, the "nothings" of the world if we are not to miss the important things.

GLOSSARY

activism. Meaningful action in support of social change.

aesthetic. Cultural shaping of modes—beauty.

affect. Feeling, emotion, intangible sensation.

affective intensities. Flows of feeling.

agentive. Having agency, moving into active mode.

anthropology. Study of people, places, and phenomena through participant observation.

arts practice. Doing art in the world, associated with practice as research.

autonomous models. Skills-based conceptualizations of literacy associated with formal schooling.

collaboration. Doing things together, working together.

coproduction. Making things together.

creativity. Activity associated with newness, transformation, stretching of possibility.

critical literacy. Questioning approach to literacy texts.

critical race theory. Thinking about power structures within education, predicated upon an understanding of inequality through racism.

defamiliarization. Process that prompts people to reimagine things and events in a different, unfamiliar light.

dissensus. Divergence that is productive.

divergence. Moving apart for productive changes.

embodiment. Process of working through and with the body.

emergence. Process of things coming into being.

everyday. Lives as lived, embodied, and culturally shaped in communities.

fractal. Dividing up equally, as a tree might.

haptic. Gestural—moving with nonverbal gestures.

ideological models. Understandings of literacy rooted in power structures and cultural forms.

(im)material. Referring to materiality that is not seen, invisible.

inscription. Writing or drawing on objects or surfaces.

interdisciplinary. Involving multiple disciplines that cross into one another and mingle.

literacy. Communicational practices that includes script, talk and other modal forms.

literacy event. Moment where literacy is involved in an activity.

literacy hubs. Places that involve varied forms of literacy texts and practices in the broadest sense.

literacy practice. Recurring moment, literacy as settled in time and space.

mark making. Making lines, patterns, and textures on artwork materials or surfaces.

materiality. Things that are in the world, observable, felt, taking up space.

multimodality. Meaning making as practiced across drawing, writing, gesture, visual, and other sensory activities and modes.

new materialism. Turn to seeing the vibrancy in matter and its agency.

"not yet." Emergent understanding of practices.

posthuman. Referring to how humans are not the sole beings in the world and to the importance of the nonhuman.

public pedagogies. Moments of learning in spaces that are outside school, commonly associated with museums.

reflexivity. Ways in which researchers' own perceptions and thoughts are bound up with their research.

scaffolding. A term from Vygotksy to describe the work of enabling an action to happen.

scalar movements. Movements by individuals across time and space based on dynamic hierarchies of privilege and status.

schooled literacy activities. Literacy-based activities presented in schools, such as spelling tests.

singularity. Moment to rest and draw together, point of convergence.

social hermeneutics. Reading the meaning in everyday, finding in the everyday a textual source of meaning.

speculative thinking. Thinking informed by process philosophy focused on emergence.

synesthesia. Mixing of senses as individuals interact and engage with texts.

tacit modalities. Ways to describe how objects hold thoughts, feelings, senses, and affective intensities.

techné. Derived from Aristotelian philosophy referring to craft. It is a way of describing design work honed with time, experience, and technical expertise.

transliteracies. Literacy practices that move across time and space in fluid and complex ways.

text. Something bound together in space and time to make meaning.

utopian. Concerned with a better life and hopeful practice.

"What if … ?" Dynamic and vital thinking during making, thinking, and literacy work.

worldmaking. Symbolic and practical work to make meaning through and beyond technology.

APPENDIX: FEATURED RESEARCH STUDIES

CHAPTER 2 FEATURED STUDY

"Rolling in the Deep: Seeing Differently"

- **Funder:** James Hugh Corcoran Memorial Trust Fund, Brock University's Social Justice Research Institute
- **Team:** Jennifer Rowsell, Terry Trzecak, Glenys McQueen-Fuentes, Kari-Lynn Winters, Susan Venditti, and Aaron Wagner
- **Location:** Niagara region, Ontario, Canada
- **Time frame:** June–July 2016
- **Participants:** Eleven adults who frequented Start Me Up Niagara
- **Intent:** To use and apply arts-based practices with adults who experience mental health issues, drug or alcohol addiction, or any combination of these
- **Activities:**
    - *Project 1:* Photograph objects in community or community hubs, as well as random objects.
    - *Project 2:* Engage in movement exercises, story-making and tableau work.
    - *Project 3:* Engage in story building and mask making
- **Outcomes:** Staged celebration and mounted art exhibit at Start Me Up Niagara in St. Catharines

CHAPTER 3 FEATURED STUDIES

"Imagine"

- **Funder:** Economic and Social Research Council
- **Team:** Kate Pahl, Zanib Rasool, Shaheen Shah, Zahir Rafiq, Paul Ward, Elizabeth Campbell, Eric Lassiter, Elizabeth Pente, and Miles Crompton
- **Location:** Rotherham, United Kingdom
- **Time frame:** January 2012–December 2017
- **Participants:** Women's writing group, women's group in a community library, girls' poetry group
- **Intent:** To help young people explore imagining better communities through artwork, poetry, and creative writing
- **Activities:** Worked on coproducing projects with community groups. Conducted oral history and creative writing
- **Outcomes:** Cocreated poetry and artwork. Coauthored book (Campbell et al. 2018).

"Making Meaning Differently"

- **Funder:** Arts and Humanities Research Council (AHRC)
- **Team:** Kate Pahl, Steve Pool, Steve Connelly, and Dave Vanderhoven
- **Location:** Rotherham, United Kingdom
- **Time frame:** November 1, 2012–April 30, 2013
- **Participants:** Fifteen to twenty young people, aged 14–24
- **Intent:** To help young people explore their perceptions of government
- **Activity:** Worked on coproducing film that expressed their feelings
- **Outcomes:** Presented film to government civil service. Coauthored book chapter (Pool and Pahl 2015)

"Research Rebels"

- **Funder:** Inspire Rotherham
- **Team:** Kate Pahl and Chloe Allan
- **Location:** Rotherham, United Kingdom
- **Time frame:** June 2009–April 2011
- **Participants:** Ten to fifteen young people, aged 8–16
- **Intent:** To help young people research what their library means to them

- **Activity:** Worked on coproducing film about their library
- **Outcomes:** Showed film to senior library staff. Coauthored article (Pahl and Allan 2011)

"Threads of Time" (also featured in chapter 4)

- **Funder:** AHRC
- **Team:** Zanib Rasool, Shahin Shah, Kate Pahl, and Helen Mort
- **Location:** Rotherham, United Kingdom
- **Time frame:** March–July 2016
- **Participants:** Eight to nine young women, aged 13–18, and poet Helen Mort
- **Intent:** To help young women explore their experiences and reimagining of future
- **Activity:** Worked on cowriting poems in response to discussions
- **Outcome:** Coproduced book of poems

CHAPTER 4 FEATURED STUDIES

"Communicating Wisdom: Fishing and Youth Work"

- **Funder:** AHRC
- **Team:** Johan Siebers, Kate Pahl, Richard Steadman-Jones, Steve Pool, Hugh Escott, and Marcus Hurcombe
- **Location:** Rotherham, United Kingdom
- **Time frame:** January 2012–December 2013
- **Participants:** Youth service and angling organization
- **Intent:** To help young people, aged 11–15, explore wisdom of fishing through intergenerational coaching and philosophy
- **Activities:** Worked on coproducing projects with community groups. Conducted oral history and creative writing
- **Outcomes:** Cocreated poetry and artwork. Coauthored book chapter (Pahl, Escott, et al. 2017)

"Community Arts Zone"

- **Funder:** Social Sciences and Humanities Research Council of Canada (SSHRC)
- **Team:** Jennifer Rowsell, Kate Pahl, Steve Pool, and Abigail Hackett

- **Location:** Rotherham, United Kingdom
- **Time frame:** 2014–2016
- **Participants:** Young children and their parents and carers at a playground
- **Intent:** To engage in immersive work using cardboard boxes and art practices as methodology
- **Activity:** Codeveloped immersive understanding of arts
- **Outcome:** Coauthored article (Hackett, Pahl, and Pool 2018)

"A Leap of Faith"

- **Funder:** AHRC
- **Team:** Steve Pool, Kate Pahl, Johan Siebers, and Patrick Meleady
- **Location:** Rotherham, United Kingdom
- **Time frame:** March–July 2016
- **Participants:** Adventure playground and playworkers, children
- **Intent:** To explore utopian nature of play
- **Activities:** Made a film about utopia and play
- **Outcomes:** Coconstructed pirate ship and coproduced books from school and women's group

"Writing in the Home and in the Street"

- **Funder:** AHRC
- **Team:** Kate Pahl, Richard Steadman-Jones, Steve Pool, William Gould, Irna Qureshi, and Zahir Rafiq
- **Location:** Rotherham, United Kingdom
- **Time frame:** October 2010–November 2011
- **Participants:** Six young people, aged 9–13
- **Intent:** To help young people explore what writing means to them
- **Activities:** Worked on repurposing toddler book for teenagers and on putting together exhibition
- **Outcomes:** Mounted exhibition in central Sheffield art gallery. Authored book (Pahl 2014a)

CHAPTER 5 FEATURED STUDY

"Visualizing Families"

- **Funder:** Brock University's Social Justice Research Institute (Community Engagement Grant)

- **Team:** Diane Collier and Jennifer Rowsell
- **Location:** Niagara region, Ontario, Canada
- **Time frame:** January–June 2016
- **Participants:** Class of grade 4 students, aged 8–9, and their teacher
- **Intent:** To explore nature and properties of arts inquiry by helping children tell stories about their families through their family photographs
- **Activities:** Worked with elementary school students as they engaged and played with family photos online and on paper, with and without technology
- **Outcome:** Authored article (Collier 2019)

CHAPTER 6 FEATURED STUDIES

"Odd: Feeling Different in the World of Education"

- **Funder:** AHRC
- **Team:** Kate Pahl, Steve Pool, Rachel Holmes, Amanda Ravetz, Becky Shaw, and Jo Ray
- **Location:** Manchester, United Kingdom
- **Time frame:** February 2018–February 2021
- **Participants:** Whole elementary school, specifically, grade 4 students, aged 8–9
- **Intent:** To help elementary school students research what "odd" means to them
- **Activities:** Worked on coproducing set of films about "feeling odd" and making "Odd Boxes."
- **Outcomes:** Presented films both indoors and outdoors

"Language as Talisman"

- **Funder:** AHRC
- **Team:** Kate Pahl, Hugh Escott, Jane Hodson, Richard Steadman-Jones, David Hyatt, Steve Pool, and Marcus Hurcombe
- **Location:** Rotherham, United Kingdom
- **Time frame:** February–November 2012
- **Participants:** Two grade 5 classes of students, aged 9–10
- **Intent:** To help elementary school students research what language means to them

- **Activities:** Worked on coproducing set of films about language
- **Outcomes:** Presented films. Coauthored article (Escott and Pahl 2017)

"A Reason to Write" (also featured in chapter 4)

- **Funder:** UK Creative Partnerships Programme
- **Team:** Kate Pahl and Steve Pool
- **Location:** Thurnscoe, South Yorkshire, United Kingdom
- **Time frame:** 2011–2012
- **Participants:** Six elementary school students, aged 10–11
- **Intent:** To help young people research impact of artists in their school
- **Activity:** Conducted analytic discussion about writing
- **Outcome:** Coauthored article (Pahl and Pool 2011)

"Taking Yourselves Seriously" (also featured in chapters 3 and 4)

- **Funder:** AHRC
- **Team:** Kate Pahl, Zanib Rasool, Andrew McMillan, Steve Pool, Mike Fitter, and Katy Goldstraw
- **Location:** Rotherham, United Kingdom
- **Time frame:** January 2017–February 2019
- **Participants:** Adventure playground, school, and group of Muslim Pakistani–heritage women
- **Intent:** To explore impact of artistic methods on social cohesion
- **Activities:** Worked on coconstructing pirate ship in playground., coproducing book, cowriting poetry and cocreating artwork
- **Outcomes:** Coconstructed pirate ship and coproduced books from school and women's group

CHAPTER 7 FEATURED STUDIES

"Maker Literacies"

- **Funder:** SSHRC
- **Team:** Jennifer Rowsell, Amélie Lemieux, Larry Swartz, Jennifer Burkitt, Peter Vietgen, Jason Hawreliak, Ann Rigg, Vanessa Crosbie-Ramsay, Melissa Turcotte, and Tara Markovitch
- **Location:** Niagara region, Ontario, Canada
- **Time frame:** March 2017–March 2021

- **Participants:** Five elementary and high school classes of students, aged 7–16
- **Intent:** To help cross-sector professionals and educators coteach teenage students by focusing on one mode of expression and representation (i.e., film, graphic texts, coding, game design, or photography)
- **Activities:**
    - *Project 1:* "Documentary Filmmaking"—produce theme-based documentary on topics such as homelessness, PTSD, addiction, and war or genocide.
    - *Project 2:* "Graphic Story and Animated Film"—design and produce cartoons, graphic stories, and animated film based on same story.
    - *Project 3:* "Coding"—learn basics and advanced schemes of coding and apply them to own digital story.
    - *Project 4:* "Game Design"—develop board game concept on future careers, then design it, conduct usability tests, develop marketing pitch, and present final product at *Dragons' Den* event.
- **Outcomes:** Coproduced MP4 documentary *Maker Literacies* (https://tinyurl.com/makerliteraciesdocumentary). Presented board game at *Dragons' Den* event. Mounted "Face Value: An Exploration of the Self Portrait through a Multimodal Lens" art exhibit at Rodman Hall Art Centre, Brock University. Coauthored two book chapters (Lemieux and Rowsell 2019a, 2019b) and two refereed journal articles (Rowsell, Lemieux, et al. 2018; Rowsell and Shillitoe 2019)

"Makerspace Research Days"

- **Funder:** Brock University's Faculty of Education (Research and Development Fund)
- **Team:** Jennifer Rowsell, Candace Figg, Kim Pelchat, and Shannon Welbourn
- **Location:** Niagara region, Ontario, Canada
- **Time frame:** January–May 2017
- **Participants:** Forty undergraduate education students, twenty teacher education students, and faculty members
- **Intent:** To set up, host, and facilitate three makerspace Saturday events throughout an academic semester

- **Activities:** Makerspace station activities included green screen; woodwork; Makey Makey and music composition; sewing and fabric work; coding; robots; virtual reality and gaming; beadwork; and arts and crafts with glue guns
- **Outcome:** Authored article (Rowsell 2020)

"Resettled Literacies"

- **Funder:** SSHRC
- **Team:** Jennifer Rowsell and Julianne Burgess
- **Location:** Niagara region, Ontario, Canada
- **Time frame:** January–April 2018
- **Participants:** Fifteen refugees receiving services at Niagara Folk Arts Multicultural Centre
- **Intent:** To apply arts-based and multimodal teaching methods with refugees in order to help them both improve their literacy and linguistic skills and acquire more expansive view of language teaching and learning
- **Activities:**
    - *Project 1:* "Language and Visual Work"—have critical discussions and undertake arts-based practices with conceptual photographs.
    - *Project 2:* "Selfies with Wordles"—produce self-portraits.
    - *Project 3:* "Every Object Tells a Story"—bring in valued object and write narrative about it.
    - *Project 4:* "Animoto/Photo Collage"—use Animoto software to produce collage about resettlement story.
    - *Project 5:* "Poetry and Similes"—retell story in native language and then turn it into poem. Pair up with partner and write down poem and its approximate English translation. Cut out phrases from poem and have partner create similes from them in English
- **Outcome:** Coauthored article (Burgess and Rowsell 2020)

REFERENCES

Abrams, S. S. 2014. *Integrating virtual and traditional learning in 6–12 classrooms: A layered literacies approach to multimodal meaning making*. New York: Routledge.

Abrams, S. S., and Rowsell, J. 2019. Immateriality redux: Tacit modalities and meaning across timescales. In D. Pyles, R. Rish, H. Pleasants, and J. Warner, eds., *Negotiating place and space in digital literacies: Research and practice*, 241–259. Charlotte, NC: Information Age.

Ahmed, S. 2004. *The cultural politics of emotion*. Edinburgh: University of Edinburgh Press.

Ahmed, S. 2006. *Queer phenomenology: Orientations, objects, others*. Durham: Duke University Press.

Ahmed, S. 2014. *The cultural politics of emotion*. 2nd ed. New York: Routledge.

Ahmed, S. 2017. *Living a feminist life*. Durham: Duke University Press

Akhtar, P. 2014. "We were Muslims but we didn't know Islam": Migration, Pakistani Muslim women and changing religious practices in the UK. *Women's Studies International Forum*, 47, 232–238.

Alaimo, S., and Hekman, S., eds. 2008. *Material feminisms*. Bloomington: Indiana University Press.

Anderson, C. 2012. *Makers: The new industrial revolution*. New York: Crown Business.

Back, L. 2007. *The art of listening*. London: Berg.

Bakhtin, M. M. 1981. *The dialogic imagination*. Edited by M. Holquist. Austin: University of Texas Press.

Banks, S., Armstrong, A., with Booth, M., Brown, G., Carter, K., Clarkson, M., Corner, L., Genus, et al. 2014. Using co-inquiry to study co-inquiry: Community-university perspectives on research. *Journal of Community Engagement and Scholarship* 7 (1): 37–47.

Banks, S., Hart, A., Pahl, K., and Ward, P., eds. 2019. *Co-producing research: A community development approach.* Bristol: Policy Press.

Barad, K. 2003. Posthumanist performativity: Toward an understanding of how matter comes to matter. *Journal of Women in Culture and Society* 28 (3): 801–831.

Barad, K. 2007. *Meeting the universe halfway: Quantum physicals and the entanglement of matter and meaning.* Durham: Duke University Press.

Barone, T., and Eisner, E. 2012. *Arts based research.* London: Sage.

Barrett, E., and Bolt, B., eds. 2010. *Practice as research: Approaches to creative arts enquiry.* London: Tauris. First published in 2007.

Barton, D. 1994. *Literacy: An introduction to the ecology of the written language.* Oxford: Blackwell.

Barton, D., and Hamilton, M. 1998. *Local literacies: Reading and writing in one community.* London: Routledge.

Barton, D., and Hamilton, M. 2000. Literacy practices. In D. Barton, M. Hamilton, and R. Ivanič, eds., *Situated literacies: Reading and writing in context,* 7–15. New York: Routledge.

Beavis, C. 2014a. Games as text, games as action: Videogames in the English classroom. *Journal of Adult and Adolescent Literacy* 57 (6): 433–439.

Beavis, C. 2014b. Video games and electronic media. In P. Albers, T. Holbrook, and A. S. Flint eds., *New methods in literacy research,* 210–223. London: Routledge.

Beck, C., and Gleyzon, F. 2016. Deleuze and the event(s). *Journal for Cultural Research* 20 (4): 329–333. https://doi.org/10.1080/14797585.2016.1264770.

Bell, D., and Pahl, K. 2018. Co-production: Towards a utopian approach. *International Journal of Social Research Methodology* 21 (1): 105–117.

Bennett, J. 2010. A vitalist stopover on the way to a new materialism. In D. Coole and S. Frost eds., *New materialisms: Ontology, agency, and politics,* 47–69. Durham: Duke University Press.

Berger, J. 1972. *Ways of seeing.* London: Penguin.

Berlant, L. and Stewart, K. 2019 *The hundreds.* Durham: Duke University Press.

Bhabha, H. 1994. *The location of culture.* London: Routledge

Bhabha, H. 2009. In the cave of making: Thoughts on third space. In K. Ikas and G. Wagner eds., *Communicating in the third space,* ix–xiv. London: Routledge.

Blackburn, M., and Clark, C., eds. 2007. *Literacy research for political action and social change*. New York: Peter Lang.

Bloch, E. (1918) 2000. *The spirit of utopia*. Translated by A. A. Nassar. Stanford: Stanford University Press. Originally published as *Geist der Utopie*.

Bloch, E. (1930) 2006. *Traces*. Translated by A. A. Nassar. Stanford: Stanford University Press. Originally published as *Spuren*.

Bloch, E. (1954) 1986. *The principle of hope*. Vol. 1. Translated by N. Plaice, S. Plaice, and P. Knight. Oxford: Blackwell. Originally published as *Das Prinzip Hoffnung*, vol. 1.

Bloome, D., and Green, J. 2015. The social and linguistic turns in studying language and literacy. In J. Rowsell and K. Pahl, eds., *The Routledge handbook of literacy studies*, 19–34. London: Routledge.

Blommaert, J., and Backus, A. 2012. Superdiverse repertoires and the individual. In I. Saint-Georges and J. Weber, eds., *Multilingualism and multimodality: The future of education research*, 1–32. Rotterdam: Sense.

Boggs, G. L., Duarte, R., and Manglitz, J. 2017. Orality as cultural action—Contributions to literacy. *Writing & Pedagogy* 9 (1): 21–47.

Braidotti, R. 2013. *The posthuman*. Cambridge: Polity Press.

Brandt, D. 2001. *Literacy in American lives*. Cambridge: Cambridge University Press.

Brandt, D., and Clinton, K. 2002. Limits of the local: Expanding perspectives on literacy as a social practice. *Journal of Literacy Research* 34 (3): 337–356.

Bruner, J. 1960. *The process of education*. Cambridge, MA: Harvard University Press.

Burgess, J., and Rowsell, J. 2020. Transcultural-affective flows and multimodal engagements: Reimagining pedagogy and assessment with adult language learners. *Language and Education*. Published online January 31. https://doi.org/10.1080/09500782.2020.1720226.

Burke, K. 1954. *Permanence and change: An anatomy of purpose*. Los Altos, CA: Hermes.

Burnard, P., Craft, A., and Cremin, T., with Duffy, B., Hanson, R., and Keene, R. 2006. Documenting possibility thinking: A journey of collaborative inquiry. *International Journal of Early Years Education* 14 (3): 243–262.

Burnett, C. 2015. (Im)materialising literacies. In J. Rowsell and K. Pahl, eds., *The Routledge handbook of literacy studies*, 520–531. London: Routledge.

Burnett, C., Davies, J., Merchant, G., and Rowsell, J. 2014. *New literacies around the globe*. London: Routledge.

Burnett, C., and Merchant, G. 2018. Literacy-as-event: Accounting for relationality in literacy research. *Discourse: Studies in the Cultural Politics of Education*. Published online April 6. https://doi.org/10.1080/01596306.2018.1460318.

Burnett, C., Merchant, G., Pahl, K., and Rowsell, J. 2014. The (im)materiality of literacy: The significance of subjectivity to new literacies research. *Discourse: Studies in the Cultural Politics of Education* 35 (1): 90–103.

Campbell, E., and Lassiter, L. E. 2010. From collaborative ethnography to collaborative pedagogy: Reflections on the other side of Middletown Project and community/university research partnerships. *Anthropology and Education Quarterly* 41 (4): 370–385.

Campbell, E., and Lassiter, L. E. 2015. *Doing ethnography today: Theoretical issues and pragmatic concerns.* Oxford: Wiley-Blackwell.

Campbell, E., Pahl, K., Pente, E., and Rasool, Z., eds. 2018. *Re-imagining contested communities: Connecting Rotherham through research.* Bristol: Policy Press.

Carter, P. 2004. *Material thinking.* Melbourne: Melbourne University Publishing.

Collier, D. 2015. "I'm just trying to be tough, okay?": Masculine performances of everyday practices. *Journal of Early Childhood Literacy* 15 (2): 203–226.

Collier, D. 2019. Re-imagining research partnerships: Thinking through "co-research" and ethical practice with children and youth. *Studies in Social Justice* 13 (1): 40–58.

Comber, B. 2016. *Literacy, place and pedagogies of possibility.* London: Routledge.

Compton-Lilly, C. 2010. Considering time in the field of family literacy and in the lives of families. In K. Dunsmore and D. Fisher, eds., *Bringing literacy home,* 306–331. Newark, DE: International Reading Association.

Compton-Lilly, C. 2015. Longitudinal studies and literacy studies. In J. Rowsell and K. Pahl, eds., *The Routledge handbook of literacy studies,* 218–230. New York: Routledge.

Connelly, S., Vanderhoven, D., Durose, C., Richardson, L., and Matthews, P. 2015. Translation across borders: Exploring the use, relevance and impact of academic research in the policy process. In P. Matthews and D. O'Brien, eds., *After urban regeneration: Communities, policy and place,* 181–198. Bristol: Policy Press.

Cope, B., and Kalantzis, M. 2000. Multiliteracies: The beginning of an idea. In B. Cope and M. Kalantzis, eds., *Multiliteracies: Literacy learning and the design of social futures,* 3–8. London: Routledge.

Corcoran, S. 2010. Editor's introduction. In J. Rancière, *Dissensus: On politics and aesthetics,* ed. and trans. S. Corcoran, 1–26. London: Continuum Press.

Covino, W. 1988. *The art of wondering: A revisionist return to the history of rhetoric.* Portsmouth, NH: Boynton/Cook.

Craft, A. R. 2013. Childhood, possibility thinking and wise, humanising educational futures. *International Journal of Educational Research* 61:126–134.

Crescenzi, L., Jewitt, C., and Price, S. 2014. The role of touch in preschool children's learning using iPads versus paper interactions. *Australian Journal of Language and Literacy* 37 (2): 86–95.

Crisco, V. 2009. Activating activist literacy: Discovering dispositions for civic identity development. *Composition Studies* 37 (2): 31–51.

Dahya, N. 2017. Critical perspectives on youth digital media production: "Voice" and representation in educational contexts. *Learning, Media and Technology* 42 (1): 100–111. https://doi.org/10.1080/17439884.2016.1141785.

Daniel, J. O., and Moylan, T., eds. 1997. *Not yet: Reconsidering Ernst Bloch*. London: Verso.

Dawkins, R. 1976. *The selfish gene*. Oxford: Oxford University Press.

Delagrange, S. H. 2011. *Technologies of wonder: Rhetorical practice in a digital world*. Logan: Utah State University Press.

Dewey, J. 1902. *The child and the curriculum*. Chicago: University of Chicago Press.

Dolan, J. E. 2016. Splicing the divide: A review of research on the evolving digital divide among K–12 students. *Journal of Research on Technology in Education* 48 (1): 16–37.

Donaldson, J. 2014. The maker movement and the rebirth of constructionism. *Hybrid Pedagogy*. Published online January 23. https://hybridpedagogy.org/constructionism-reborn/.

Dyson, A. H. 2003. *The brothers and sisters learn to write*. New York: Teachers College Press.

Dyson, A. H. 2008. Staying in the (curricular) lines: Practice constraints and possibilities in childhood writing. *Written Communication* 25 (1): 119–159.

Ehret, C. 2018a. Moments of teaching and learning in a children's hospital: Affects, textures, and temporalities. *Anthropology & Education Quarterly* 49 (1): 53–71.

Ehret, C. 2018b. Propositions from affect theory for feeling literacy through the event theoretical models and practices of reading. In D. E. Alvermann, N. J. Unrau, M. Sailors, and R. B. Ruddell, eds., *Theoretical models and processes of literacy*. 7th ed., 563–581.New York: Routledge.

Ehret, C., Hollett, T., and Jocius, R. 2016. The matter of new media making: An intra-action analysis of adolescents making a digital book trailer. *Journal of Literacy Research* 48 (3): 346–377.

Eliot, G. (1871) 1965. *Middlemarch*. London: Penguin.

Ellsworth, E. 2005. *Places of learning: Media, architecture, pedagogy*. New York: Routledge.

Enriquez, G., Johnson, E., Kontavourki, S., and Mallozzi, C., eds. 2016. *Literacies, learning and the body: Putting theory and research into pedagogical practice*. London: Routledge.

Escott, H. and Pahl, K. 2017. Learning from ninjas: Young people's films as a lens for an expanded view of literacy and language. *Discourse: Studies in the Cultural Politics of Education* 40 (6): 805–815. Published online November 24. https://doi.org/10.1080/01596306.2017.1405911.

Facer, K., and Pahl, K., eds. 2017. *Valuing collaborative interdisciplinary research: Beyond Impact.* Bristol: Policy Press

Figg, C., Pelchat, K., Rowsell, J., and Welbourne, S. 2018. Pop-up makerspaces: A pilot study of makerspace take up. Research and development grant funded by the Brock University Faculty of Education, St. Catharines, Ontario, Canada.

Finnegan, R. 2015. *What is language?* London: Routledge

Foucault, M. 1980. *Power/knowledge: Selected interviews and other writing, 1972–1977.* Edited by C. Gordon. Translated by C. Gordon, L. Marshal, J. Mepham, and K. Soper. New York: Pantheon Books.

Gee, J. P. 2004. *Situated language and learning: A critique of traditional schooling.* New York: Routledge.

Georgakopoulou, A. 2007. *Small stories, interactions, and identities.* Amsterdam: John Benjamins.

Georgakopoulou, A. 2015. Small stories research. In A. D. Fina and A. Georgakopoulou, eds., *The handbook of narrative analysis,* 255–271. Hoboken, NJ: Wiley.

Gilbert, J. 2014. *Common ground: Democracy and collectivity in an age of individualism.* London: Pluto Press.

Gillborn, D., and Ladson-Billings, G. 2010. Critical race theory. In P. Peterson, E. Baker, and B. McGaw, eds., *International encyclopedia of education.* 3rd ed., 341–347. Oxford: Elsevier.

Greene, M. 2000. *Releasing the imagination: Essays on education, the arts and social change.* New York: Teachers College Press. First published in 1993.

Grenfell, M., and Pahl, K. with McClean, C., Compton-Lilly, C., and Seloni, L. L. 2019. *Bourdieu, language-based ethnographies and reflexivity: Putting theory into practice.* New York: Routledge.

Grosz, E. 2005. *Time travels: Feminism, nature, and power.* Durham: Duke University Press.

Gutiérrez, K. D. 2016. Designing resilient ecologies: Social design experiments and a new social imagination. *Educational Researcher* 45 (3): 187–196. Originally presented in 2011. https://www.researchgate.net/profile/Kris_Gutierrez2/publication/301570696_2011_AERA_Presidential_Address_Designing_Resilient_Ecologies_Social_Design_Experiments_and_a_New_Social_Imagination/links/5a66f539aca2720ba6b030b3/2011-AERA-Presidential-Address-Designing-Resilient-Ecologies-Social-Design-Experiments-and-a-New-Social-Imagination.pdf.

Hackett, A. 2014. Zigging and zooming all over the place: Young children's meaning making and movement in the museum. *Journal of Early Childhood Literacy* 14 (1): 5–27.

Hackett, A., Pahl, K., and Pool, S. 2018. In amongst the glitter and the squashed blueberries: Crafting a collaborative lens for children's literacy pedagogy in a community setting, *Pedagogies: An International Journal* 12 (1): 58–73.

Halverson, E. R., and Sheridan, K. M. 2014. The maker movement in education. *Harvard Educational Review* 84 (4): 495–504.

Hamdi, N. 2004. *Small Change: About the art of practice and the limits of planning in cities*. London: Earthscan.

Hamilton, M. 2012. *Literacy and the politics of representation*. London: Routledge.

Hanny, C., Duckles, J., Smith, J., Moses, R., and Greenwich, G. J. 2018. When theory met practice: Methodology in the versus. In J. Larson, and G. Moses, eds., *Community literacies as shared resources for transformation*, 35–54. New York: Routledge.

Haraway, D. 2008. *When species meet*. Minneapolis: University of Minnesota Press.

Hart, A., Davies, C., Aumann, K., Wenger, E., Aranda, K., Heaver, B., and Wolff, D. 2013. Mobilising knowledge in community-university partnerships: What does a community of practice approach contribute? *Contemporary Social Science: Journal of the Academy of Social Sciences* 8 (3): 278–291.

Harwood, D. and Collier, D. 2017. The matter of the stick: Storying/re-storying children's literacies in the forest. *Journal of Early Childhood Literacy* 17 (3): 336–352.

Harwood, V., Hickey-Moody, A., McMahon, S., and O'Shea, S., eds. 2017. *The politics of widening participation and university access for young people: Making educational futures*. London: Routledge.

Hauge, C. 2014. Youth media and agency. *Discourse: Studies in the Cultural Politics of Education* 35 (4): 471–484. https://doi.org/10.1080/01596306.2013.871225.

Hayles, N. K. 2008. *How we became posthuman: Virtual bodies in cybernetics, literature, and infomatics*. Chicago: Chicago University Press.

Heath, S. B. 1983. *Ways with words: Language, life and work in communities and classrooms*. Cambridge: Cambridge University Press.

Heath, S. B., Street, B. V., with Mills, M. 2008. *On ethnography: Approaches to language and literacy research*. New York: Teachers College Press.

Hickey-Moody, A. 2013. *Youth, arts and education*. Abingdon, UK: Routledge.

Hicks, D. 2002. *Reading lives: Working-class children and literacy and learning*. New York: Teachers College Press.

Hill, M. L., and Vasudevan, L., eds. 2008. *Media, learning and sites of possibility*. New York: Peter Lang.

Hoggart, R. 1957. *The uses of literacy*. London: Penguin.

hooks, b. 1984. Black women: Shaping feminist theory. In *Feminist theory: From margin to center*, 1–17. Boston: South End Press.

Hull, G. A., and Nelson, M. E. 2009. Literacy, media and morality: Making the case for an aesthetic turn. In M. Baynham and M. Prinsloo, eds., *The future of literacy studies*, 199–228. Basingstoke, UK: Palgrave.

Hultman, K., and Lenz Taguchi, H. 2010. Challenging anthropocentric analysis of visual data: A relational materialist methodological approach to educational research. *International Journal of Qualitative Studies in Education* 23 (5): 525–542.

Hyatt, S. 2014. Making history through community action. Paper presented at the Imagine: Second Annual Conference. Huddersfield, UK, September.

Hyatt, S. 2017. Community histories. Paper presented at the Imagine Community Research Day. Rotherham, UK, June.

Hymes, D., ed. 1996. *Ethnography, linguistics, narrative inequality: Towards an understanding of voice*. London: Routledge.

Ingold, T. 2007. *Lines: A brief history*. Abingdon, UK: Routledge.

Ingold, T. 2008. Bindings against boundaries: Entanglements of life in an open world. *Environment and Planning* 40 (8): 1796–1810.

Ingold, T. 2013. *Making: Anthropology, archaeology, art and architecture*. Abingdon, UK: Routledge.

Ingold, T. 2014. That's enough about ethnography! *Journal of Ethnographic Theory* 4 (1): 383–395

Jackson, A., and Mazzei, L. 2012. *Thinking with theory in qualitative research: Viewing data among multiple perspectives*. London: Routledge.

Jenkins, H. 2006. *Convergence culture: Where old and new media collide*. New York: New York University Press.

Jenson, J., Dahya, N. and Fisher, S. 2014. Valuing production values: A "do it yourself" media production club. *Learning, Media and Technology* 39 (2): 215–228.

Jones, S. 2006. *Girls, social class and literacy*. Portsmouth, UK: Heinemann.

Jónsdóttir, S. R., and Gunnarsdóttir, R. 2017. *The road to independence: Emancipatory pedagogy*. Rotterdam: Sense.

Kafai, Y. B., Fields, D. A., and Searle, K. A. 2014. Electronic textiles as disruptive designs: Supporting and challenging maker activities in schools. *Harvard Education Review* 84 (4): 532–556.

Kell, C. 2006. Crossing the margins: Literacy, semiotics and the recontextualisation of meanings. In K. Pahl and J. Rowsell, eds., *Travel notes from the New Literacy Studies: Instances of practice*, 147–172. Clevedon, UK: Multilingual Matters.

Kinloch, V. 2010. *Harlem on our minds*. New York: Teachers College Press.

Knobel, M. 2006. Memes and affinity spaces: Some implications for policy and digital divides in education. *E-Learning* 3 (3): 411–427.

Knobel, M., and Lankshear, C. 2007. Online memes, affinities, and cultural production. In M. Knobel and C. Lankshear, eds., *A new literacies sampler*, 199–227. New York: Peter Lang.

Kress, G. 1997. *Before writing: Rethinking the paths to literacy*. New York: Routledge Press.

Kress, G. 2010. *Literacy in the new media age*. New York: Routledge.

Kuby, C. R., and Gutshall Rucker, T. 2016. *Go be a writer!: Expanding the curricular boundaries of literacy learning with children*. New York: Teachers College Press.

Kuby, C. R., Gutshall Rucker, T., and Kirchhofer, J. M. 2015. "Go be a writer": Intra-activity with materials, time and space in literacy learning. *Journal of Early Childhood Literacy,* 15 (3), 394–419.

Kuby, C. R., and Rowsell, J., eds. 2017. Early literacy and the posthuman: Pedagogies and methodologies. Introduction to special issue. *Journal of Early Childhood Literacy* 17 (3): 285–296.

Kuby, C. R., Spector, K., and Thiel, J. 2018. *Posthumanism and literacy education: Knowing/becoming/doing literacies*. New York: Routledge.

Kuhn, A. 2010. Memory texts and memory work: Performances of memory in and with visual media. *Memory Studies* 3 (4): 298–313.

Kumasi, K. D. 2011. Critical race theory and education: Mapping a legacy of scholarship and activism. In B. A. U. Levinson with J. P. K. Gross, C. Hanks, J. H. Dadds, K.D. Kumasi, J. Link, and D. M. Roland, eds., *Beyond critique: Critical social theories and education*, 196–219. Boulder, CO: Paradigm.

Ladson-Billings, G., and Tate, W. E. 1995. Towards a critical race theory of education. *Teachers College Record* 97 (1): 47–68.

Larson, J. 2014. *Radical equality in education: Starting over in U.S. schooling*. New York: Routledge.

Larson, J., and Moses, G. H., eds. 2018. *Community literacies as shared resources for transformation*. New York: Routledge.

Lassiter, E. 2005. *The Chicago guide to collaborative ethnography*. Chicago: University of Chicago Press.

Lassiter, L. E., Goodall, H., Campbell, E., and Johnson, M. N., eds. 2004. *The other side of Middletown: Exploring Muncie's African American community*. Walnut Creek, CA: Altamira Press.

Leander, K. M., and Boldt, G. M. 2013. Rereading "a pedagogy of multiliteracies": Bodies, texts, and emergence. *Journal of Literacy Research* 45 (1): 22–46.

Leander, K. M., and Ehret. C., eds. 2019. *Affect in literacy learning and teaching pedagogies, politics and coming to know*. London: Routledge

Leander, K. M., and Sheehy, M. 2004. *Spatializing literacy research and practice*. New York: Peter Lang.

Leander, K. M., and Wells Rowe, D. 2006. Mapping literacy spaces in motion: A rhizomatic analysis of a classroom literacy performance. *Reading Research Quarterly* 41 (4): 428–460.

Lee, C. 2003. Why we need to re-think race and ethnicity in educational research. *Educational Researcher* 32 (5): 3–5.

Lefebvre, H. (1974) 1991. *The production of space*. Translated by D. Nicholson-Smith. 2nd ed. Oxford: Wiley-Blackwell. Originally published as *La production de l'espace*.

Lemke, J. 2000. Across the scales of time: Artifacts, activities, and meanings in ecosocial systems. *Mind, Culture, and Activity* 7 (4): 273–290.

Lenz Taguchi, H. 2011. Investigating learning, participation and becoming in early childhood practices with a relational materialist approach. *Global Studies of Childhood* 1 (1): 36–50.

Lewis, C., and Tierney, J. 2013. Mobilizing emotion in an urban classroom: Producing identities and transforming signs in a race-related discussion. *Linguistics and Education* 23:289–304.

MacLure, M. V. 2011. Qualitative inquiry: Where are the ruins? *Qualitative Inquiry* 17 (10): 997–1005.

MacLure, M. V. 2016. The refrain of the a-grammatical child: Finding another language in/for qualitative research. *Cultural Studies—Critical Methodologies* 16 (2): 173–182.

Madison, D. S. 2011. *Critical ethnography: Method, ethics, and performance*. Los Angeles: Sage.

Mahuika, R. 2008. Kaupapa Māori theory is critical and anti-colonial. *MAI Review* 3 (article 4): 1–16.

Marsh, J., Kumpulainen, K., Nisha, B., Velicu, A., Blum-Ross, A., Hyatt, D., et al. 2017. *Makerspaces in the early years: A literature review*. Sheffield, UK: University of Sheffield MakEY Project.

Massey, D. 2005. *For space*. London: Sage.

Massumi. B. 2011. *Semblance and event*. Cambridge, MA: MIT Press.

Massumi, B. 2015. *Politics of affect*. Malden, MA: Polity Press.

Mavers, D. 2011. *Children's drawings and writing: The remarkable in the unremarkable*. Abingdon, UK: Routledge.

Maybin, J. 2013. Working towards a more complex sociolinguistics. *Journal of Sociolinguistics* 17 (4): 547–555.

McLean, C. 2019. Insider identities: Coming to know the ethnographic researcher. In M. Grenfell and K. Pahl, eds., *Bourdieu, Language-based ethnographies and reflexivity: Putting theory into practice*, 91–106. New York: Routledge.

Merleau-Ponty, M. (1945) 1962. *Phenomenology of perception*. Translated by C. Smith. New York: Humanities Press. Originally published as *Phénomenologie de la perception*.

Merleau-Ponty, M. (1948) 2004. *The world of perception*. Translated by O. Davis. New York: Routledge. Originally published as *Causeries*.

MHCLG (Ministry of Housing, Communities and Local Government). 2018. *Integrated communities strategy green paper*. London: HM Government. https://assets.publishing.service.gov.uk/government/uploads/system/uploads/attachment_data/file/696993/Integrated_Communities_Strategy.pdf.

Miller, D. 2008. *The comfort of things*. Hoboken, NJ: Wiley.

Mitchell, C. 2011. *Doing visual research*. Los Angeles: Sage

Morrell, E. 2008. *Critical literacy and urban youth: Pedagogies of access, dissent, and liberation*. New York: Routledge.

Morrell, E. 2017. Toward equity and diversity in literacy research, policy, and practice: A critical, global approach. *Journal of Literacy Research* 49 (3): 454–463.

Morrell, E. and Rowsell, J., eds. 2019. *Stories from inequity to justice in literacy education: Confronting digital divides*. New York: Routledge.

Moses, G., Larson, J., Duckles, J., Galegos Greenwich, J., Moses, R., Van Alstyne, et al. 2018. Our research team's statement of unity of values in unpredictable times. In J. Larson and G. Moses, eds., *Community literacies as shared resources for transformation*, ix–x. New York: Routledge.

Mouffe, C. 2007. Artistic activism and agonistic spaces. *Art and Research* 1 (2). Published online in summer 2007. http://www.artandresearch.org.uk/v1n2/mouffe.html.

My ECE Experts. 2013–2019. Te Whariki: What is this early childhood "curriculum" that ECE services are required by the Ministry of Education to follow? https://www.myece.org.nz/educational-curriculum-aspects/106-te-whariki-curriculum.

Nagar, R. 2014. *Muddying the waters: Coauthoring feminisms across scholarship and activism*. Urbana: University of Illinois Press.

Nelson, M. E., Hull, G., and Young, R. 2013. Portrait of the artist as a younger adult: Multimedia literacy and "effective surprise." In O. Erstad and J. Sefton-Green, eds., *Identity, community and learning lives in the digital age*, 215–232. Cambridge: Cambridge University Press.

Neuman, S. and Celano, D. 2013. *Giving our children a fighting start: Poverty, literacy and the development of information capital*. New York: Teachers College Press.

New London Group. 1996. A pedagogy of multiliteracies: Designing social futures. *Harvard Educational Review* 66 (1): 60–92.

Niagara Connects. 2014. Living in Niagara 2014: Critical indicators for reflecting on life in Niagara. http://www.livinginniagarareport.com/wp-content/uploads/Living_In_Niagara_2014_summary_booklet.pdf.

Nichols, S. M., Rowsell, J., Nixon, H., and Rainbird, S. 2012. *Resourcing early learners: New networks, new actors*. New York, Routledge.

Nirantar Collective. 2007. *Exploring the everyday: Ethnographic approaches to literacy and numeracy*. New Delhi: Nirantar.

Norquist, B. 2017. *Literacy and mobility: Complexity, uncertainty, and agency at the nexus of high school and college*. New York: Routledge.

Pahl, K. 1999. *Transformations*. Stoke on Trent, UK: Trentham Books.

Pahl, K. 2002. Ephemera, mess and miscellaneous piles: Texts and practices in families. *Journal of Early Childhood Literacy* 2 (2): 145–166.

Pahl, K. 2012 "A reason to write": Exploring writing epistemologies in two contexts. *Pedagogies: An International Journal* 7 (3): 209–228

Pahl, K. 2014a. *Materializing literacies in communities: The uses of literacy revisited*. London: Bloomsbury.

Pahl, K. 2014b. The aesthetics of everyday literacies: Home writing practices in a British Asian household. *Anthropology and Education Quarterly* 45 (3): 293–311.

Pahl, K. 2019. Recognizing young people's civic engagement practices: Rethinking literacy ontologies through co-production. *Studies in Social Justice* 13 (1): 20–39.

Pahl, K., and Allan, C. 2011. "I don't know what literacy is": Uncovering hidden literacies in a community library using ecological and participatory research methodologies with children. *Journal of Early Childhood Literacy* 11 (2): 190–213.

Pahl, K., Escott, H., Siebers, J., and Steadman-Jones, R., with Simmons, J., Hurcombe, M., Kirsty, and Anglers from Phoenix and Parkgate Junior Angling Club. 2017. Fishing and youth work, or "What is it about fishing that makes life better?" In C. Walker, A. Hart, and P. Hanna, eds., *Building a new community psychology of mental health: Spaces, places, people and activities*, 83–100. Basingstoke, UK: Palgrave Macmillan.

Pahl, K., and Khan, A. 2015. Artifacts of resilience: Enduring narratives, texts, practices across three generations. In J. Sefton-Green and J. Rowsell, eds., *Learning and literacy over time: Longitudinal perspectives*. New York: Routledge.

Pahl, K., and Pool, S. 2011. "Living your life because it's the only life you've got": Participatory research as a site for discovery in a creative project in a primary school in Thurnscoe, UK. *Qualitative Research Journal* 11 (2):17–37.

Pahl, K., and Pool, S. 2018. Re-imagining artistic subjectivities within community projects. *Open Library of Humanities* 4 (2): 1–22. https://doi.org/10.16995/olh.248/.

Pahl, K. and Rowsell, J. 2006. *Travel notes from the New Literacy Studies: Instances of practice*. Clevedon, UK: Cromwell Press.

Pahl, K., and Rowsell, J. 2010. *Artifactual literacies: Every object tells a story*. New York: Teachers College Press.

Papert, S.1980. *Mindstorms: Children, computers and powerful ideas*. New York: Basic Books.

Papert, S. 1993. *Mindstorms: Children, computers, and powerful ideas*. 2nd ed. New York: Basic Books.

Pente, E., Ward, P., Brown, M., and Singh, H. 2015. The coproduction of historical knowledge: Implications for the history of identities, identity papers. *Journal of British and Irish Studies* 1 (1): 32–53.

Peppler, K. A., and Bender, S. 2013. Maker movement spreads innovation one project at a time. *Phi Delta Kappan* 95 (3): 22–27.

Perry, M., Collier, D., and Rowsell, J. 2019. Reframing the digital in literacy: Youth, arts, and misperceptions. In E. Morrell & J. Rowsell, eds., *Stories from inequity to justice in literacy education: Confronting digital divides*, 71-86. New York, NY: Routledge.

Pink, S. 2006. *Doing visual ethnography*. 2nd ed. London: Sage.

Pink, S. 2009. *Doing sensory ethnography*. London: Sage.

Pink, S. 2011. Sensory digital photography: Re-thinking moving and the image. *Visual Studies*, 26 (1): 4–13.

Pink, S., and Leder Mackley, K. 2014. Reenactment methodologies for everyday life research: Art therapy insights for video ethnography. *Visual Studies* 29 (2): 146–154.

Pool, S. 2018. *Everything and nothing is up for grabs: Using artistic methods within participatory research*. Connected Communities Programme. Bristol: University of Bristol.

Pool, S., and Pahl, K. 2015. The work of art in the age of mechanical co-production. In D. O'Brien and P. Mathews, eds., *After urban regeneration: Communities, policy and place*, 79–94. Bristol: Policy Press.

Potter, J., and McDougall, J. 2017. *Digital media, culture and education: Theorising third space literacies*. Basingstoke, UK: Palgrave Macmillan.

Rancière, J. 2010. *Dissensus: On politics and aesthetics*. Edited and translated by S. Corcoran. London: Continuum.

Rasool, Z. 2017. Collaborative working practices: Imagining better research partnerships. *Research for All* 1 (2): 310–322.

Rasool, Z. 2019. Faith, culture and identity: The everyday literacy practices. In D. Bloome, M. L. Castanheira, C. Leung, and J. Rowsell, eds., *Re-theorizing literacy practices: Complex social and cultural context*. New York: Routledge.

Rautio, P. 2013. Children who carry stones in their pockets: On autotelic material practices in everyday life. *Children's Geographies* 11 (4): 394–408. https://doi.org/10.1080/14733285.2013.812278.

Ravetz, J. and Ravetz, A. 2016. Seeing the wood from the trees: Social Science 3.0 and the role of visual thinking. *Innovation: European Journal of Social Science* 30 (1): 104–120.

Reddo-Lodge, R. 2017. *Why I am no longer talking to white people about race*. London: Bloomsbury.

Richardson, W. 2007. In search of further education of youth in post-war England. *Journal of Vocational Education & Training* 59 (3): 385–418.

Rockhill, K. 1987. Language and the politics of literacy. *British Journal of Sociology* 8 (2): 153–167

Rogers, R. 2018. *Reclaiming powerful literacies: New horizons for critical discourse analysis*. New York: Routledge.

Rose, G. 2010. *Doing family photography: The domestic, the public and the politics of sentiment*. Surrey, UK: Farnham.

Rose, G. 2012. *Visual methodologies: An introduction to researching with visual materials*. Thousand Oaks, CA: Sage.

Rotas, N., and Springgay, S. 2013. "You go to my head": Art, pedagogy and a "politics-to-come." *Pedagogies: An International Journal* 8 (3): 278–290.

Rowsell, J. 2013. *Working with multimodality: Rethinking literacy in a digital age*. London: Routledge.

Rowsell, J. 2014. "The mood is in the shot": The challenge of moving-image texts to multimodality. *Talk and Text* 34 (3): 307–324.

Rowsell, J. 2020. "How emotional do I make it?": Making a stance in multimodal compositions. *Journal of Adolescent & Adult Literacy*. Published online January 10. https://doi.org/10.1002/jaal.1034.

Rowsell, J., Lemieux, A., Swartz, L., Turcotte, M., and Burkitt, J. 2018. The stuff that heroes are made of: Elastic, sticky, messy literacies in children's transmedial cultures. *Language Arts* 96 (1): 7–20. http://dc.msvu.ca:8080/xmlui/bitstream/handle/10587/1926/ALemieux_Sticky_article.pdf.

Rowsell, J., and McQueen-Fuentes, G. (2017). Moving parts in imagined spaces: Community arts zone's movement project. *Pedagogies: An International Journal* 12 (1): 74–89.

Rowsell, J. and Pahl, K. 2007. Sedimented identities in texts: Instances of practice. *Reading Research Quarterly* 42 (3): 388–404.

Rowsell, J., and Shillitoe, M. 2019. The craftivists: Pushing for affective, materially informed pedagogy. *British Journal of Educational Technology* 50 (4): 1544–1559. https://doi.org/10.1111/bjet.12773.

Rowsell, J., and Vietgen, P. 2017. Embracing the unknown in community arts zone visual arts. *Pedagogies: An International Journal* 12 (1): 90–107.

Schrock, A. 2014. "Education in disguise": Culture of a hacker and maker space. *InterActions: UCLA Journal of Education and Information Studies* 10 (1): 1–25. http://escholarship.org/uc/item/0js1n1qg.

Scollon, R., and Scollon, S. W. 2003. *Discourses in place: Language in the material world*. London: Routledge.

Sefton-Green, J., and Rowsell, J., eds. 2015. *Learning and literacy over time: Longitudinal perspectives*. New York: Routledge.

Shah, S. 2018. Silk and steel. In E. Campbell, K. Pahl, E. Pente, and Z. Rasool, eds. 2018, *Re-imagining contested communities: Connecting Rotherham with research*, 53–58. Bristol: Policy Press.

Shillitoe, M. 2018. Post-digital learning, technology, and the media educator. Master's research diss., Piet Zwart Institute, Rotterdam.

Shklovsky, V. 1917. Art as technique. https://muratgermen.files.wordpress.com/2009/11/art-as-technique.pdf. First published in 1925 as chapter 1 in Shklovsky's essay collection *О теории прозы* (*Theory of Prose*).

Shusterman, R. 2012. *Thinking through the body: Essays in somaesthetics*. Cambridge: Cambridge University Press.

Siegel, M. 2006. Rereading the signs: Multimodal transformations in the field of literacy education, *Language Arts* 84 (1): 65–77.

Soja, E. 2010. *Seeking spatial justice*. Minneapolis: University of Minnesota Press.

Springgay, S., and Rotas, N. 2014. How do you make a classroom operate like a work of art? Deleuzeguattarian methodologies of research-creation. *International Journal of Qualitative Studies in Education* 28 (5): 552–572. https://doi.org/10.1080/09518398.2014.933913.

Springgay, S., and Truman, S. 2018. On the need for methods beyond proceduralism: Speculative middles, (in) tensions and response-ability in research. *Qualitative Inquiry* 24 (3): 203–214.

Stein, P. 2008. Multimodal instructional practices. In J. Coiro, M. Knobel, C. Lankshear, and D. Leu, eds., *Handbook of research on new literacies*, 871–898. New York: Erlbaum.

Stewart, K. 2007. *Ordinary affects*. Durham: Duke University Press.

Stornaiuolo, A. 2015. Literacy as worldmaking: Multimodality, creativity and cosmopolitanism. In J. Rowsell and K. Pahl, eds., *The Routledge handbook of literacy studies*, 561–572. Abingdon, UK: Routledge.

Stornaiuolo, A., and Jung, J. K. 2017. Public engagement and digital authoring: Korean adolescents write for/as action. In R. Zaidi and J. Rowsell, eds., *Literacy lives in transcultural times*, 102–116. New York: Routledge.

Stornaiuolo, A., and LeBlanc, R. J. 2016. Scaling as literacy activity: Mobility and educational inequality in an age of global connectivity. *Research in the Teaching of English* 50 (3): 263–287.

Stornaiuolo, A., Smith, A., and Phillips, N. 2017. Developing a transliteracies framework for a connected world. *Journal of Literacy Research* 49 (1): 68–91.

St. Pierre, E. A. 2011. Anything can happen and does. *Critical Studies—Critical Methodologies*, (4): 386–389.

Street, B. V. 1984. *Literacy in theory and practice*. Cambridge: Cambridge University Press.

Street, B. V., ed. 1993a. *Cross-cultural approaches to literacy*. Cambridge: University of Cambridge Press.

Street, B. V. 1993b. Culture is a verb: Anthropological aspects of language and cultural process. In D. L. Gradoll, L. Thompson, M. Byrem, and J. K. Cowan, eds., *Language and culture*. Clevedon, UK: Ball and Multilingual Matters.

Street, B. V. 1995. *Social literacies*. London: Longman.

Street, B. V. 1997. The implications of New Literacy Studies for literacy education. *English in Education* 31 (3): 26–39.

Street, B. V. 2010. Academic literacies approaches to genre? *Revista Brasileira de Linguística Aplicada* 10 (20): 347–361. Originally presented in 2009.

Taylor, C. 2004. *Modern social imaginaries*. Durham: Duke University Press.

Tett, L., Hamilton, M., and Crowther, J., eds. 2012. *More powerful literacies*. Leicester, UK: NIACE.

Thiel, J. J. 2015. "Bumblebee's in trouble!" Embodied literacies during imaginative superhero play. *Language Arts* 93 (1): 38–49.

Tilley, S. A. 2016. *Doing respectful research: Power, privilege and passion*. Halifax, NS: Fernwood.

Truman, S. 2019. Inhuman literacies and affective refusals: Thinking with Sylvia Wynter and secondary school English. *Curriculum Inquiry* 49 (1): 110–128. https://doi.org/10.1080/03626784.2018.1549465.

Tuhiwai Smith, L., Tuck, E., and Yang, W. K. 2019. *Indigenous and decolonizing studies in education: Mapping the long view*. New York: Routledge.

Vasudevan, L. 2011. An invitation to unknowing. *Teachers College Record* 113 (6): 1154–1174.

Vasudevan, L., and DeJaynes, T. 2013. Becoming "not yet": Adolescents making and remaking themselves in art-full spaces. In L. Vasudevan and T. DeJaynes, eds., *Arts, media, and justice: Multimodal explorations with youth*, 1–26. New York: Peter Lang.

Walsh, M., and Simpson, A. 2013. Touching, tapping … thinking? Examining the dynamic materiality of touch pad devices for literacy learning. *Australian Journal of Language and Literacy* 36 (3): 148–157.

Walton, I., and Cotton, C. (1653) 2008. *The compleat angler*. Oxford: Oxford University Press.

Ward, C. 1973. *Anarchy in action*. London: Freedom Press.

Weber, S. 2012. Visual images in research. In J. G. Knowles and A. L. Cole, eds., *Handbook of the arts in qualitative research: Perspectives, methodologies, examples, and issues*, 2–13. Thousand Oaks, CA: Sage. https://doi.org/10.4135/977914452226545.

Wenger, E. 1998. *Community of practice: Learning, meaning and identity*. Cambridge: Cambridge University Press.

Werbner, P. 1990. *The migration process: Capital, gifts and offering among British Pakistani*. New York: St. Martin's Press.

Whitty, P. 2015. Complicating literacies: Settler ways of being with story(ies) on Wabanaki lands. In R. Zaidi and J. Rowsell, eds. 2017. *Literacy lives in transcultural times*. Expanding Literacies in Education Series. New York: Routledge.

Williams, R. (1958) 1989. *Resources of hope: Culture, democracy, socialism*. London: Verso.

Williams, R. 1961. *The long revolution*. London: Chatto & Windus.

Willis, P. 2000. *The ethnographic imagination*. Cambridge: Polity Press.

Wissman, K., Staples, J. M., Vasudevan, L., and Nichols, R. E. 2015. Cultivating research pedagogies with adolescents: Created spaces, engaged participation, and embodied inquiry. *Anthropology & Education Quarterly* 46 (2): 186–197.

Wohlwend, K. E. 2015. One screen, many fingers: Young children's collaborative literacy play with digital puppetry apps and touchscreen technologies. Digital media and literacies special issue. *Theory into Practice* 54 (2): 154–162.

Yeats, W. B. 1962. *Poems of W. B. Yeats*. Edited by A. N. Jeffries. London: Macmillan.

INDEX